CW01476329

BERNADOTTE

BERNADOTTE

Marshal of France
& King of Sweden

Lord Russell of Liverpool

ASCENT BOOKS

Printed in Great Britain by
Butler & Tanner Limited
Frome & London
ISBN 0 86254 004 6

Contents

Preface

Although Bernadotte was always considered in northern Europe as one of the best kings Scandinavia ever had, there has nearly always been in France a kind of malediction on him. It cannot be denied that after he had received many favours from Napoleon, Bernadotte became his enemy, and that sufficed for him to be regarded in the country of his birth as a traitor. It is not perhaps surprising, when one realises that even today Napoleon is regarded by a majority of his countrymen as the greatest of them all, that because of this many of them are unable to see the wood for the trees. Until comparatively recently Bernadotte has never had a fair trial and most Frenchmen have been inclined to find him guilty before they have heard all the evidence. When writing this book I have, therefore, tried to keep this in mind.

One famous French historian, however, writing some years ago passed this judgement on him.

> 'The story of Bernadotte is like a fairy story. A native of the Béarn, grandson of a tailor in Pau and son of a lawyer in the same town, he became a Marshal of France, Prince of Ponte-Corvo, the Crown Prince of Sweden, and, eventually, its King. But he was not the kind of king that Napoleon's brothers and Murat were—they did not keep their crowns for very long. Bernadotte, however, was the founder of a dynasty to which the kings of Sweden have

belonged up to this present day. This may seem like a miracle but it was due to the fact that he possessed a rare combination of qualities: intelligence, courage, a chivalrous charm and a natural majesty.'[1]

CHAPTER ONE

Before the Revolution

On 26 January 1763 Bernadotte was born at Pau where his father was a lawyer. His birth was premature and for a few weeks it was not expected that he would live.

Pau is the principal town in the old province of Béarn. Although outside the geographical boundaries of the old Gascony, the Béarnais, as the inhabitants of the Béarn are still known, were Gascons, but they had certain characteristics of their own, and no two Béarnais were, in some respects, more alike than Henry IV and Bernadotte.[1]

Even their homes were in sight of each other. Henry IV was born in the Chateau and Bernadotte in a small house in the town a few hundred yards below. They both became kings, yet at the time of their birth there was no likelihood that either of them would ascend a throne.

Bernadotte was called by many Frenchmen *un vrai Gascon* and in some ways he was. One of his characteristics was boastfulness, and the definition of Gascon in the *Concise Oxford Dictionary* is 'braggart'. It must be said in Bernadotte's favour, however, that he certainly had a great deal to boast about from the early days of his life until his death in Sweden after reigning for twenty-five years.

Another resemblance was that each of them changed their religion to become king. Lastly they each started new dynasties which endured for generations—Bernadotte's family is still the reigning dynasty in Sweden.

It was always the intention of Bernadotte's father that his son should be called to the Bar, and at the age of fourteen he became a student and a clerk in the office of Maître Jean Pierre de Batsalle, who was a procureur in the Parliament of Navarre.

There is a certain amount of evidence that his childhood was not very happy, one of the reasons being that his elder brother was his mother's favourite. This might not have affected him as much as it appears to have done had he not been a weakly child, which made him extremely sensitive. In spite of this he always remained fond of his mother. There was one thing, however, which he was quite certain about and that was that he did not want to be called to the Bar. It was not surprising, therefore that shortly after his father died on 31 March 1780, when Bernadotte was still only seventeen years old, he left home with the intention of joining the army.

His choice of regiment was based solely on the fact that there was a local recruiting officer of the Regiment Royal-la-Marine, but there was still one obstacle which he managed to overcome without any difficulty. Under the Army Regulations his formal document of enlistment had to have the visa of a civil authority and if he had gone to the local Mairie the news would probably have reached his family.

He was able to have the document signed by the Maire of another Commune not far away from Pau.

The Royal-la-Marine was a regiment of light infantry which had only been formed eighteen years previously, with a regimental depot situated at Collioure on the Mediterranean coast. It was, of course, to the regimental depot that

Bernadotte was first sent as a recruit and thence, after a few weeks' training, he joined the regiment itself, at that time stationed at Toulon. Very soon afterwards it was sent to Bastia in Corsica which had only been part of France for twelve years and still needed a garrison to keep order; there was considerable discontent among the inhabitants of the island with whom the transfer of Corsica from Genoa to France was not at all popular. His first experiences of army life were not too pleasant, for the conditions in the barracks in Bastia could not have been worse; even the NCOs slept two in a bed.

After he had served for two years he became entitled to six months leave which he spent in Pau with his mother. While there he became quite ill as a result of which he got two extensions of leave and spent about eighteen months in Pau before finally returning to his regiment.

During this time his mother did everything she could to get him to try and buy himself out of the army and continue his legal studies. He had found his first two years in the service hard going and had it not been for a duel with a young police officer in Lesear whom he wounded, and which made it necessary for him to get away from Pau as quickly as possible, he might not have rejoined his regiment. According to some of his biographers, and these have been many, he spent most of his leave improving his knowledge by reading many books, particularly those on military history.

There is ample confirmation that the illness which enabled him to get two extensions of leave was quite genuine, since he suffered very much during the early years of his life from lung trouble for which the climate of Pau, which lies at the foot of the Pyrenees, is excellent. Bad health had affected his studies as a schoolboy. He realised this and welcomed the opportunity during his sick-leave to catch up with his knowledge of history.

The Regiment Royal-la-Marine, just after Bernadotte rejoined, left Corsica to form part of the garrison in Grenoble. By this time the French army had been cut down by about half which naturally made a considerable reduction in the opportunities for promotion. Nevertheless, during the first year after returning to his regiment, he was promoted twice: in June 1785 he became a Corporal and two months later he was made a Sergeant. It had taken him five years to reach that rank. Although he did not apparently correspond regularly with his family, the following letter which he wrote to his brother, seven months after his promotion, is of some interest:

> 'My dear brother,
>
> 'I have received your letter.... They have made me several offers which they have promised to take the first opportunity of putting into effect.... I look forward to some more settled position because, I must confess, my present condition is full of ups and downs. In truth there are only a few enjoyable moments to compensate for the anxieties which the service exacts. Eight days ago I returned from Avignon, where I was sent on duty, in pursuit of a young man who had deserted from his regiment. I arrested him alone in the presence of nine soldiers of the Toulon Marines who were conducting him to their corps. I received the praise of the Major of my Regiment and of all the officers. They have held out hopes that I shall receive a gratuity on the occasion of the Review. I have certainly earned it well. In three months I have effected three arrests. In two cases the fugitives were within half an hour of Chambéry, which is on the frontier.... If I

become a Sergeant-Major, as they lead me to hope, I shall receive at least thirty-two sols (halfpence) a day ... I am for life your devoted brother.

Bernadotte,
Sergeant of Light Infantry

'Grenoble 9 March 1786. Give my respects to my dear mother, and my love to my sister.'

It was in fact almost two years before he was promoted to the rank of Sergeant-Major, but during that period he received the appointment of 'fourrier écrivant' which is roughly the equivalent of a Company Quarter-Master Sergeant, although it does not carry with it any special rank. He was duly promoted Sergeant-Major on 11 May 1788, slightly less than a month before he became involved in a confrontation between his regiment and some of the revolutionary inhabitants of Grenoble as a result of a riot which took place on 7 and 8 June 1788. The troops were called out to deal with the disturbance and a number of the rioters climbed on the roofs of some of the houses and threw tiles at the soldiers, hence its name, *La Journée des Tuiles*. This confrontation made the Regiment Royal-la-Marine very unpopular and four months later at the request of the local Parliament it was moved to Vienne, south of Lyons.

Early in September 1789 it once again moved, this time to Marseilles where Bernadotte's future wife, Désirée Clary, lived. She was the daughter of François Clary, a rich businessman, and Bernadotte's first visit to her father's house has been described by Désirée as follows:

'One day a soldier presented himself with a requisition billeting him in our house at Marseilles. My father, who had no wish to be disturbed by the noise which soldiers usually make, politely sent him back with a letter to his colonel requesting that an officer might be billeted on us instead of a soldier. The soldier who was sent back in this way was Bernadotte, who was afterwards to marry me and become a King.'[2]

CHAPTER TWO

From NCO to Sub-Lieutenant

By this time Bernadotte had been in the Army for nine years and was regarded by his colonel and many of the other officers of his battalion as a very competent NCO and suitable for promotion to commissioned rank. He was extremely smart in his appearance and was generally known as 'Sergeant Belle-jambe'. In February 1790 he was appointed to the post of Adjutant, the highest position which could be held by an NCO.

Shortly after this appointment, when the battalion was being inspected by General the Marquis de Boutilliers, he told the battalion commander that if their adjutant was as smart as he looked he was a credit to the regiment. 'I can assure you', the colonel replied, 'that his smart appearance is the least of his merits.' The colonel was the Marquis d'Ambert whose life Bernadotte was to save on 20 March 1790.

By this time the French Revolution had really begun, and on 15 May 1789 the deputies of what was known as the Third Estate proclaimed themselves to be the National Assembly; from then onwards there was a revolutionary feeling throughout France. With the exception of Paris, no town was more revolutionary than Marseilles where Bernadotte's regiment was stationed. Ever since the fall of the Bastille on 14 July 1789 there had been considerable ill feeling between the king's army and the new forces which had been formed in nearly all the large municipalities and were called the National Guard.

In Marseilles the corps of National Guardsmen was very large and continually patrolled the city, so it was not likely to be long before there was an open clash. On 20 March 1790 Colonel d'Ambert, who had been to Avignon for a few days, returned urgently to Marseilles because he had been informed that there was trouble in the city. When he arrived at one of the city gates he was stopped by a National Guard sentry.

An account of the incident was adopted by a committee of the National Assembly which considered a report on the matter that had been submitted to them. The greater part of it was reported in *Le Moniteur* in its issue of 29 March 1790.

> 'The sentry asked for the names of the occupants of the Colonel's carriage but d'Ambert refused to give any information and pretended not to know anything about the National Guard when the sentry said that it was to them he belonged and that he had every right and authority to stop any person entering through one of the city gates.'

Colonel d'Ambert, according to the National Guard sentry, was very rude but eventually, in the words of the report, 'd'Ambert appealed to the regular guard who identified him as Colonel of the Regiment Royal-la-Marine'. As there had been a regular army sentry there all the time, there would appear to have been no need for this fracas to have taken place at all, and the fact that it did confirms the animosity which the revolutionary National Guard felt against the regular army.

It was also reported in this issue of *Le Moniteur* that before Colonel d'Ambert told his driver to carry on he called the National Guardsmen *canailles* or rabble, and said that with one company of his battalion he could wipe out their whole corps and that they might take that message to the mayor and the municipality.

On the following day Bernadotte was at the City Hall with a number of his fellow NCOs, in order to try to come to some agreement with the municipality and persuade them that in future the National Guard should treat the regular troops more as comrades than as enemies. Colonel d'Ambert arrived at the City Hall surrounded by a crowd who were threatening to hang him on the nearest lamp post.

Bernadotte rescued his commanding officer from the murderous mob by haranguing them. Later on in life he made many famous speeches but this one is the first on record. 'Citizens of Marseilles', he is reported to have said, 'surely you do not wish to stain the honour of your city by assassination. If the Colonel has done wrong, let the law, of which your magistrates are the guardians, judge him. If, however, you attempt any illegal violence against him it will be over the dead bodies of myself and my comrades.'[1]

Bernadotte's appeal was successful. Colonel d'Ambert was temporarily saved from the guillotine—but only for eight years. The matter was, however, referred to the National Assembly by one of the Marseilles deputies. Bernadotte and his fellow NCOs were able to send a full statement which was also considered by the Assembly, and which Bernadotte, in a covering letter, described as an accurate account of the events of what by then was referred to as the 'affaire d'Ambert'. The covering letter was as follows:

> 'The non-commissioned officers of the Regiment Royal-la-Marine have the honour to address to you an accurate account of the unhappy occurence which has befallen their Colonel on the occasion of his arrival in the City Hall, where he had gone in order to support the declaration which his non-commissioned officers had just made to make clear to the people their ardent wishes for union and

> peace.... We beg of you, M. le President, and we dare to hope from your kindness and goodness, that you will suspend all judgement until the reports have reached you from both sides. We have the honour to be, M. le President, your very humble and obedient servants the non-commissioned officers of the Regiment Royal-la-Marine—Bernadotte, Adjutant.'[2]

The letter was also signed by eleven other NCOs.

The municipality succeeded in getting Bernadotte's regiment moved from Marseilles because of this incident and by 21 April 1790 the Regiment Royal-la-Marine was garrisoned in a town called Lambesc where, according to a report in *Le Moniteur*, there was nearly a mutiny in the regiment. A large number of soldiers, who had now begun to catch the revolutionary fever, held a meeting in the church which was being temporarily used as a barracks and proposed to elect their senior non-commissioned officer, L'Adjutant Bernadotte, commander of the Regiment Royal-la-Marine. When this happened Bernadotte is said to have gone up into the pulpit, thanked his comrades for having paid him such a compliment, after which he succeeded in convincing them that no soldier of the king could be a party to such a mutiny.

The regiment only remained in Lambesc for a very short time after which it went to the Isle de Ré. The situation in France was becoming worse every day, although it must have been very evident to Bernadotte, who was nothing if not intelligent, that promotion was not far away. The first opportunity came in 1792 when he was still in Ré and expected to be elected by the regiment to a sub-lieutenancy but, to his great surprise and annoyance, he did not obtain a majority of the votes. (At that time, under a revised military law, most lieutenants and sub-lieutenants were elected by regimental officers.)

What he felt was expressed in a letter to his brother:

'... There has been an election to a sub-lieutenancy for which I failed to get a majority of votes. A sergeant-major, a gentleman whom I myself promoted to the rank, obtained more votes than I did. Nevertheless all the officers expressed to me their regret at having had to yield to certain considerations, and assured me that in the promotion which must soon take place, I shall have the first choice of appointment. I have not been deluded by these empty promises, and I have not allowed them to ignore the injustice which they have done me. I have put forward the good order and discipline of the 1st Battalion which is the result of my personal work. I reproached some of these gentlemen with their ingratitude. The dangers and risks which I have run on their account were not forgotten. The Commanding Officer and Senior Captain united in assuring me that the result was contrary to their votes and they positively declared that I shall be included in the promotions which will be made at an early date. Adieu my dear brother.... To cease to love you I must cease to exist.

J. B. Bernadotte
St Martin, Isle de Ré,
23 February 1792'

The opportunity to elect Bernadotte, as his officers had promised to do, came within a very short time and he was given a commission as a sub-lieutenant. He was just about to be appointed adjutant-major of the battalion when a message was received from Paris that the Minister of War had appointed him as a lieutenant in the 36th Regiment, previously the Regiment of Anjou. By new regulations which had recently been made by the Minister of War all the old regimental names were abolished and the Royal-la-Marine was now the 60th Regiment of Infantry.

Bernadotte was informed by his CO of this appointment in a very complimentary letter in which he wrote 'your zeal for the good of the Service has been turned to the advantage of the State and has won for you the esteem of the whole corps. . . .' The way was now open for him and there must have been little doubt amongst those who had served with him during his first eleven years in the army that he would rise to great heights.

CHAPTER THREE

Rapid Promotion

It had taken Bernadotte eleven years to get a commission but it was only to take him another two years to become a colonel in command of a 'half-brigade', a unit which usually consisted of three infantry battalions and a company of artillery. Towards the end of April he joined his new regiment which was stationed in St Servan, near St Malo. Within a couple of days of his arrival war was declared and was to continue practically without cessation until the defeat of Napoleon at Waterloo on 18 June 1815.

It was Danton, who was responsible more than anyone else for starting the terrible Reign of Terror, who said, 'The limits of France are defined by nature. We shall reach them at four points—the ocean, the Rhine, the Alps and the Pyrenees'.

Shortly after Bernadotte had joined his regiment the news arrived that a French army on its way to invade Austria had, en route, lost two battles at Mons and Lille and that its commander, General Dillon, had been accused, quite unjustifiably, of treason. He was never tried for the alleged offence but was assassinated by some of his own troops and the murderous revolutionaries of Lille.

This was described in a letter which Bernadotte wrote to his brother:

> '... You know, I suppose, that the fortune of war has been against us in an opening engagement near Mons. It is said

that M. Dillon has paid with his life for either his inexperience or his treachery. I express neither blame nor approval of his conduct. Until I am better informed I suspend my judgement upon an incident which may bring in its train the greatest misfortunes. Unless the government bestirs itself to obviate the incalculable evils which license and frenzy carry in their train, punishment of this kind, which troops may claim the right to inflict on their chiefs, may deprive us of good generals as well as bad ones. . . . Having been a soldier since my boyhood I know the errors and follies of which soldiers are capable. I also know something of the way in which their affection and respect may be won when it is not too late to recall them to their duty. . . . Whatever happens I shall not desert my post; and my honour and my duty will always be my guiding motives.'

A couple of months later Bernadotte's regiment left St Servan for the front line. While he was at Mayenne—on the way to Cambraï, where a few other units were about to assemble to join the Army of the North—he wrote a letter in which he made it clear for the first time that he had fallen for the *Liberté* which was one of the three slogans of the French Revolution.

'I am delighted to enter upon active service', he wrote, 'and to fight for such a righteous cause. I have the good fortune to be in a regiment which is not divided. Discipline is regularly observed, and the purest patriotism animates them. I hope soon to be captain.' It is not improbable that the prospects of more rapid promotion in the future may have been partly responsible for his being enamoured with this new Liberty, although he states that it was not his hopes of a captaincy which pleased him so much as 'the thought of Liberty of which I know today the precious worth'.

The Reign of Terror had not quite begun but within another three months the guillotine was working overtime, and the September massacres had taken place.

Bernadotte's first General Officer Commanding was Custine, whose nick-name in the Army of the Rhine, which he commanded, was 'Le General Moustache'. His full name was General Count Adam-Phillipe de Custine de Sarrack. One of the few aristocrats who still remained in the army and had so far escaped the guillotine, he already had quite a distinguished military career including service in the American War of Independence. It was due to the fact that many aristocrats who held senior ranks in the army had already emigrated that he had been given his present command.

At the start of the campaign Custine had considerable success and after crossing the Alsatian frontier captured three important cities. He then made a serious tactical error; instead of establishing a consolidated defence line on the west bank of the Rhine, which Danton had said would remain one of France's permanent frontiers, Custine advanced across the river into Germany and was almost immediately driven back to the western bank.

Bernadotte's part in the battle brought him promotion, for he was appointed adjutant-major of his new regiment, and as a result he wrote to his brother asking him to try to obtain for him the Lieutenant-Colonelcy of a battalion. 'If you can procure my appointment to one of the battalions which is about to be formed it will suit me perfectly because, with my experience and my knowledge of the details of my profession, I hope to be able to make myself useful.'

The day after he had written this letter, Bernadotte's regiment took part in an attack which was a complete failure; some inexperienced troops fired at their own cavalry, mistaking them for Austrians, and this caused absolute chaos which was graphically described in another letter which he wrote to his brother on 26 May. After recounting how the mistake came about, he went on:

> 'while others sought safety in flight I was overwhelmed with a feeling of indignation and fury at this humiliating spectacle. Seeing no superior officer capable of restoring discipline, I rushed to the centre of the disordered battalion. I shouted, I protested, I implored, and I commanded. The noise and confusion were so great that the men could not hear me.... I rushed to the rear of the battalion, which had become the head. My horse was knocked down but I kept my position and said to the men: "Soldiers, this is the rallying point ... you will retreat no further.... Let others by a cowardly flight show themselves unworthy of liberty. Let us, if necessary, die at our post shouting *Vive la République*, *Vive la Nation*." There was an immediate response to these words, some of the soldiers saying "Let us march against the enemy led by the adjutant-major". I formed them in order of battle and checked the confusion which would have affected the other six battalions behind me.... Calm was restored, our surprise attack failed but we remained masters of the field of battle. All the officers congratulated me on my zeal and success. The soldiers speak of me with enthusiasm—but everything stops there because nobody informed the Commander-in-Chief of my conduct. The actions of subalterns often remain unnoticed whereas the mistakes of commanders pass for high achievements. However, I shall not on that account render less faithful service to the Republic to which I am devoted....'

It was not long before Custine fell. Shortly after the failure of this surprise attack he suffered defeat on the battlefield, and this time his friend and sponsor Danton was no longer in a position to defend him. Custine was tried by the Revolutionary Tribunal on a charge of treason which there was, of course, not a shred of evidence to support, but that did not prevent the Tribunal from finding him guilty. On 28 August he was guillotined.

Shortly after Custine's execution the command of the Army of the Rhine was taken over by General de Beauharnais but he did not last very long. He was no more successful than his predecessor in relieving Mainz which on 23 July 1793 had to surrender. For this failure he was never forgiven and during the Terror, which was now in full swing, he was arrested and ended up, like so many other aristocratic senior officers, at the guillotine. Ironically enough it was his widow who was later to marry Napoleon and become the Empress Josephine.

A still greater coincidence was to happen much later on. A grand-daughter of de Beauharnais eventually married Bernadotte's son Oscar and became Queen Josephine of Sweden on the death of her father-in-law in 1844.

Bernadotte had not, so far, been lucky with his generals and there was to be one more before long. He was General Houchard who had taken over command of the Army of the Rhine in succession to de Beauharnais. When the Revolutionary Tribunal sent him to the guillotine they did not even have the excuse that he was an aristocrat. He was, like Bernadotte, a man of the people but it did not help him much. It cannot be denied that he was not competent enough to hold a high command but that did not justify his being taken to the Abbaye prison where there were already twenty-four other generals, and then executed a few days later. During the short period of Houchard's command Bernadotte had been promoted captain, but three weeks later he jumped up to the rank of lieutenant-colonel in his own battalion, having been elected by 666 votes. General Jourdan now took over command and on 17 October gained an important victory at Wattignies.

Although Bernadotte had told his brother that he had begun to appreciate 'the precious worth of Liberty', he must by this time have begun to have some disillusions. The Reign of Terror had been at its height under Robespierre who had, in the words of the historian, H. A. L. Fisher, 'for every dissenter from his narrow creed, the one simple remedy of the guillotine'.[1] It was only when he went just a bit too far by passing a law which threatened the life of every member of the Convention that his end came, and, appropriately, it was in the same way as all his victims.

It was Edmund Burke, in his *Reflections on the Revolution in France*, who wrote: 'The age of chivalry has gone: that of sophisters, economists and calculators has succeeded.' At times there have been French writers who accused Bernadotte of being a revolutionary, which indeed he was in sentiment, but during the whole time these terrible events were taking place he had been a young soldier in an active regular regiment and had no responsibility whatever for the barbarous crimes and murders committed by many of the French Revolution's leaders.

That he was not going to tolerate revolutionary behaviour in his own regiment he made clear to his troops on more than one occasion. During the defence of Prémont, a fortress which covered the road to St Quentin and was attacked in April 1794 by a large force of Austrians, he pointed out the dangers of insubordination and explained that all it did was to help the enemy and shame the French army. On another occasion during the same battle, when his men started running away, he tore off his epaulettes in front of them and said, 'If you dishonour yourselves by running away I will refuse to remain your Colonel.'

Later that year Bernadotte had a narrow escape from the fate of Custine and Houchard. Apparently the Revolution leaders had been informed of what he had said to his troops at Prémont about insubordination and regarded it as 'despotic interference with the liberty of his Republican subordinates'. After he had been questioned by a delegation from an organisation called 'The Representatives of the People' an order was issued for his arrest, but it was later withdrawn. According to Touchard-Lafosse this was after the delegation had heard about the action taken by Bernadotte at Prémont when his troops began retreating. He was indeed lucky, because three other generals in the Army of the North, in which Bernadotte was then serving, were all arrested. They were all first-class generals and had committed no offence. Their only fault was that they were of Irish origin and were supposed to be royalist-minded.

One of the most important of 'The Representatives of the People' was a young man named St Just who was also more or less in control of the Committee of Public Safety, one of whose duties was to spy on the army and bring any 'disloyalists' to justice. He was perhaps the most barbarous of all the Terrorists and his score of guillotine victims was even higher than Robespierre's.

On two occasions when Bernadotte's regiment was taking part in fighting near the Belgian frontier, St Just happened to be paying a visit and had an opportunity of meeting him. St Just was so impressed that he embraced Bernadotte and then offered to have him promoted to the rank of general. He refused the offer of promotion and would in all probability have refused to be embraced, if he had been able to do so, because St Just has been described by one writer as having a 'mild mellow voice, an olive complexion and long black hair', and by another as 'having powdered hair and large blue eyes'.

Bernadotte's reason for refusing the offer of promotion was well described by General Sarrazin in his memoirs.[2]

> 'Bernadotte refused the promotion saying that he had not the talents necessary for so high a rank, and he begged the Representatives of the People to leave him in his rank of colonel in which he enjoyed the confidence of officers and men. Kleber's persuasion [General of Division Kleber] failed to shake his resolution. I was more successful, however, on a subsequent occasion. With a tone rather of regret he said to me that he had refused the rank of general because he thought himself not learned enough to fulfil the duties of that situation. I laughed heartily at his modesty, so seldom practised by the Gascons, and I assured him that, should he accept, he would be superior to several generals, whom I mentioned, and that he would have reason to regret his refusal when he found himself compelled to carry out their ill-devised orders, which would be equally injurious to his own reputation and to the service of the Republic. Having slept over my advice, he came to me next day and said, "Since such is your opinion, should I be offered again I shall accept." I communicated this avowal to Kleber.'

General Sarrazin had a high opinion of Bernadotte whom he once described as 'Gifted by nature with a handsome bearing and a commanding aspect, he was beloved by his troops because he knew all the details of his duties as commander, and was successful in looking after the well-being of his subordinates. His kindness was not more marked than his firmness in preserving discipline.'

Rapid Promotion

It was not to be long before Bernadotte won further praise on the battlefield. This was at the battle of Fleurus when he was under the command of General Jourdan; it led to the retreat of the Austrians towards the Rhine and the conquest of Belgium. The left wing of Jourdan's command, which was re-named the Army of the Sambre et Meuse, included a division commanded by General Kleber who also had a high opinion of Bernadotte and recommended him, immediately after the battle was over, for promotion to the rank of General of Brigade. The actual promotion was 'provisionally' authorised by the Representatives of the People only three days later as a reward for his bravery: *Pour bravoure et actions d'éclat*.

Bernadotte was described by an eyewitness as 'advancing, sword in hand, at the head of his troops charging the enemy's position, retaking lost ground, clearing the woods and pursuing the enemy to their camp'. Altogether three thousand prisoners were taken.

CHAPTER FOUR

Sambre et Meuse

It is generally considered that the great success of the Army of the Sambre et Meuse, which throughout the month of May had been winning victory after victory, had a considerable effect on the downfall of Robespierre and, with him, the Reign of Terror. France's enemies having been driven back from her frontiers there was nothing to justify the Terror any more. These victories which 'pursued Robespierre like the Furies' raised the morale of the French nation and when he was guillotined the same crowd which had booed his victims shouted 'Down with the tyrants: long live the Republic'.[1] France had ceased to be terrorist but she remained revolutionary.

The retreat of the Austrians after Fleurus left the way open to the Netherlands and by 6 July the French were advancing on Brussels which they took on 10 July. Bernadotte was still under Kleber's command and was always given an important role.

After the capture of Brussels the French advance continued eastward with the objective of invading western Germany and occupying the province of the Rur. To accomplish this it was necessary to cross the river of that name, known in 1794 as the Roer. Bernadotte was given the following instructions by Kleber:

'On receipt of this letter, my dear comrade, you will direct

> Adjutant-General Ney to ascertain the width of the Roer, and whether it is fordable and, if so, at what point. In any event you will requisition all procurable carpenters and collect materials for throwing a bridge across the river. Do not stand on ceremony, my dear comrade. Use, if necessary, the flooring of the houses. If you could seize Heinzberg today it would be a good step forward and a fine vanguard stroke.

Before nightfall this was all accomplished. Kleber was delighted and promised to send a report of the attack to the GOC, General Jourdan.[2] During the remainder of this campaign Bernadotte continued to go from success to success and all the generals under whose command he served had nothing but good to say of him.

It was on 2 October that the river Roer was crossed and this virtually ended the campaign. It was Bernadotte's 71st Regiment that was the first to cross, suffering a considerable number of casualties, and when it reached the other side it was able to take up a defensive position until the remainder of the Army of the Sambre et Meuse reinforced them the following day.

Kleber's despatch to the GOC about the battle gave great praise to Bernadotte. 'I cannot sufficiently praise General Bernadotte', he wrote. 'Always under heavy fire he directed the movements of his troops with heroic sang-froid. His courage and intrepidity decided the result of the battle.' A fortnight later he was recommended for promotion to General of Division. The year of 1794 had been a remarkable one for Bernadotte. From being still a captain at the beginning of the year he had become a General of Division before it ended and had been commended for his bravery and good generalship on many occasions.

The next objective of the Army of the Sambre et Meuse was to cross the Rhine but they were in an almost impossible position because they had no means of building any bridges. After crossing the Rhine they were to continue the invasion of Germany but they were without adequate supplies or sufficient reserves of ammunition.

General Jourdan summoned a meeting of all his commanders at which Bernadotte gave a very forthright opinion of the situation.

> 'Exposed as we are on the one hand to the desperate complaints of our soldiers, as a result of their sufferings and privations, and on the other hand to the malevolence of the agitators and the exacting requirements of the Government, it is better for us to perish by drowning in crossing the Rhine, or by the sword of the Austrians having crossed it, than to give the enemies of our glory a favourable opportunity of saying that we have not dared to face courageously the danger which awaits us. So far as the materials and organisation of the army are concerned, I admit the odds are all against us: but the circumstances in which we are placed leave us no alternative. If we resolutely strive for victory, she may be ours. If she should fail us, death at all events will be our refuge.'

Greatly influenced, no doubt, by this spirited speech the meeting decided to take the risk and cross the Rhine, and by 20 October the whole army were in position on the east bank of the river. At this stage of the campaign everything came to a standstill for five weeks because of a constitutional crisis involving a change in the National Convention which had governed France as a dictatorial assembly ever since the extinction of the French monarchy. The Convention had been superseded in October by an executive body known as the Directory consisting of five members elected for a term of five years. They alone had executive power though two legislative assemblies had also been created, known as The Ancients and the Five Hundred; the former had two hundred and fifty members and the latter, as its name implied, had five hundred.

One-fifth of the Directory and two-thirds of the legislature had to be re-elected or appointed each year.

This new government has been described by Albert Sorel: 'The Directory with the two councils was nothing but organised anarchy. The conquest of the natural frontiers was nothing but systematized war. War and anarchy conducted a nation, which desired order and victory, to a military dictatorship.'[3] The Directory came into existence at the end of October 1795 but it only lasted for four years.

Between the fall of the National Convention and the establishment of the Directory there was no government to give General Jourdan any orders, so he and his army had temporarily to take up a defensive position just east of the Rhine. Eventually instructions arrived for Jourdan to 'stop the enemy's advance' which he had already done, but that was all. No further supplies or ammunition were made available. The Army of the Sambre et Meuse was being so neglected by this government of regicides, by whom every general was held in suspicion, that Bernadotte gave vent to his feelings in a letter. 'I am not weak enough to wish for death but I believe that unless the Government take some severe measures a glorious death will be the greatest benefit that can befall a French general.'[4]

Another general who was also serving under Jourdan felt exactly the same as Bernadotte did. He was General Marceau and on 30 November he sent the following letter to his Commander-in-Chief:

'I am so disgusted that nothing restrains me from quitting the service and my command except my honour and my regard for you. I prefer to die in battle, even if I am alone there, rather than fail in carrying out your intentions.... I can, however, no longer place any reliance upon my troops or upon anything else except my own readiness to die.

'That is all I think I can assure you of. I have to face obstacles a hundred times more terrible than any the enemy can present. My men have neither bread nor boots, and the roads are in such a condition that the soldiers sink into the mud up to their knees.'

Both generals were thankful when, on 19 December, the Austrians proposed that there should be an armistice, a proposition which was willingly accepted. It could not have come at a better time as it gave Bernadotte an opportunity to reorganise the division and look after the welfare of his troops which was, as it is to any good commander, most important. On 21 May 1796, however, the Austrians gave notice that the armistice was to end ten days later, which gave the French army time to prepare for a further advance along the Rhine.

General Kleber's division formed the advance guard. After he had won an important victory at Altenkirchen the way was open for the rest of the army, including Bernadotte's division, to cross the Rhine at Neuwied which should have opened the way to a further advance. Unfortunately, however, Jourdan for some reason or other missed the opportunity which resulted in his army having to retreat back to the Rhine.

Bernadotte, whose division also had to retire, had received no orders from his Commander-in-Chief, as he had been expecting, and during the retreat sent the following dispatch to Jourdan:

> 'I beg of you, General, to send me orders as soon as possible. I must frankly confess that I am afraid of leaving some of my light infantry behind me. They are so scattered that I have to employ all the officers of my staff to find and collect them. Maison, who commanded a flank corps, and had to remain at Nassau until five o'clock reports that the enemy have established a bridge there.'

Having reached the Rhine, the army of the Sambre et Meuse was able to have a few days' rest behind a defensive position, and to reorganise themselves. Once again they set out to cross the Rhine at Neuwied. The attack, carried out on 22 July, was a complete success and for the following six weeks the army continued its advance into the centre of Germany.

By 10 August Bernadotte had captured Nuremberg and four days later he entered Altdorf. This was a very small town with only about a hundred inhabitants but it was of some importance as it was at that time the seat of the University of Nuremberg. The university authorities had petitioned General Jourdan and asked that the houses in which the professors lived as well as the university buildings should be exempted from billeting, and Jourdan's staff had agreed and given the university authorities a letter exempting them from billeting by 'volunteers'.

Bernadotte's officers, however, refused to act on this letter. 'We are not volunteers,' they said, 'and the letter does not refer to us'. Two professors appealed to Bernadotte whom they found engaged upon the difficult task of finding quarters for 8,000 officers and men in a place not much larger than a small village. Bernadotte was well known for leniency in dealing with the local inhabitants in countries where his troops were in occupation, but in this instance his men had to be housed and it was no hardship to the university to have to house them. The following is an account of what happened when the delegation of professors came to see Bernadotte.[5] After hearing their requests he replied: 'Very well, we won't behave in Germany as Germans have behaved in France, but mark my words: you will do as you are ordered to do, or I will have this place burnt down about your ears.'

Hans Klöber, who records the incident, comments:

> 'Considering Bernadotte's humane disposition, and in view of his behaviour to universities on later occasions, one can only assume as the reason for this scene that there was some excitement on both sides and some misunderstanding in consequence of it. With regard to the letter of protection it seems that some staff officers of Jourdan had played a joke upon the professors who wanted to study in dressing-gowns with long pipes in their mouths during the roar of the cannon, the clamour of the storming soldiers and the groaning of the wounded; and in their egotism wished, to the injury of their fellow citizens, to be free from the burden of billeting soldiers. Perhaps, too, they asked for exemption when they had not described their town at Jourdan's HQ quite in accordance with the truth. Where were the superior officers to be billeted if not in the college or in the professors' houses?'

All this did not worry Bernadotte who was just about to experience the greatest military exploit of his life, namely the raid on Ratisbon and the battle of Teining. A few days after his arrival at Altdorf he received orders to advance southwards towards Ratisbon while Jourdan with the rest of his army marched towards the frontier between Germany and Bohemia. The orders which he received were (1) to protect the right flank of the army and (2) to contact General Moreau's army which was supposed to be somewhere near the Danube. This led to Bernadotte's falling into a trap from which, due to his tactical skill, his courage and a little good luck, he was able to escape.

As the vanguard, about 9,000 strong, which he was commanding, advanced along the east bank of the river Pegnitz, a tributary of the Danube, in the direction of Ratisbon, an Austrian force of some 28,000, commanded by the Archduke Charles, advanced to meet the French. On 22 August they met at Teining where a great battle was fought.

The best description of this was written by General Sarrazin who was not only an eyewitness but took part in it.[6]

> 'Jourdan having decided upon pursuing the Austrian army ordered Bernadotte's division towards Ratisbon to endeavour to establish communication with Moreau. The Archduke Charles took a skilful advantage of the error which Jourdan committed in not marching with the whole of his troops to form a junction with the Army of the Rhine. The Archduke crossed the Danube with a chosen corps; his advanced guard attacked Bernadotte's outposts on the 21 August, and forced them to retreat upon the main position of the division encamped on the heights near the village of Teining. On 22 August the Archduke attacked the French. The engagement was a sanguinary one and success swayed to and fro during the whole day. The village of Teining was taken and retaken several times; the streets were strewn with dead bodies and towards the evening the village was set on fire, the enemy being persuaded that that

was the only means of dislodging the troops who were entrenched in the houses.

'Meanwhile the Archduke ordered his right wing to attack Bernadotte's left. The 88th Regiment of Infantry which formed part of the left wing was obliged to retreat. Bernadotte's position became most critical as the Austrians, by the advantage they had obtained, found themselves master of the main road through Neumarkt, the only way by which the French could retreat. Convinced of the necessity of retaking the ground lost by his left, Bernadotte placed himself at the head of his reserve, consisting of a battalion of Grenadiers and the 7th Regiment of Dragoons, which made up a force of about four thousand strong. He then addressed them as follows: "You know, my friends, what care I have always taken of your welfare since I had the happiness of commanding such brave fellows as yourselves. The opportunity now presents itself of testifying your grateful sense of it, of deserving well of your country and covering yourselves with glory."

'Although they had fought from daybreak and it was then nearly night these few words caused them to forget the fatigues of the day. They all exclaimed, with the greatest enthusiasm, that they were ready to follow their General to the bottomless pit of Hell. Bernadotte then gave orders to advance and marched in close column form against the centre of the enemy's line who, staggered by this daring movement, though themselves three times more numerous than their opponents, put up a very weak resistance and retired in disorder to their former position. The Archduke, despairing of carrying Bernadotte's position by main force, ordered the firing to stop and detached General Starrey's division which was threatening to turn the French left wing, whilst the columns of cavalry scoured the country upon the right wing pushing the light infantry towards Neumarkt. These movements naturally caused Bernadotte well-founded anxiety as regards his line of operations and at 10 o'clock that same night he decided to retreat from his forward position as far back as Neumarkt. During this march an accident occurred which, with less disciplined troops, might have been attended with the most fatal consequences. Towards midnight a howitzer caisson [an ammunition wagon] took fire in the centre of the column. There was a succession of explosions similar to a bombardment of artillery fire. The troops in the van and in the rear, believing that the centre of their column was being attacked, formed themselves into battle order and asked to be led forward to meet the enemy. I have often heard Bernadotte say that this confidence of the troops, notwithstanding the darkness of the night and the great losses which they had experienced earlier in the day, would always appear to him as the most pleasing moment of his life.'

CHAPTER FIVE

A Period of Discontent

General Jourdan in his memoirs wrote that Bernadotte 'with only a handful of men held his position and inflicted heavy losses on the enemy'. Furthermore in his despatch of 24 August to the Government in Paris, which was published in the issue of *Le Moniteur* for 22 September, he had stated that Bernadotte at Teining 'had given fresh proofs of his courage'.

Jourdan had, it was generally acknowledged, been largely responsible for the retreat mentioned above and it was becoming more evident every day that he was unfitted for such an important command. When the Army of the Sambre et Meuse had crossed the Rhine, after the death of Marceau from wounds sustained on 19 September, Jourdan was relieved of his command. In point of fact this is exactly what he wanted, for he had written to the government: 'I feel it my duty to inform you that the interests of the public service make it desirable that I should cease to command the Army of the Sambre et Meuse, because I have lost the confidence of my generals who no longer regard me as capable of acting as their chief.'

Both Kleber and Bernadotte held this view and the latter, who never minced his words, had expressed his view in a letter to Jourdan: 'Everybody knows that you are an honest man, a brave soldier and a good citizen, but it is in the public interest that the Government should know that you are incapable of successfully commanding as Commander-in-Chief even four men and a corporal.'

The letter containing this extract is printed in General Sarrazin's *Biographical Sketch of Bernadotte* though there is no reference to it anywhere else. Although Bernadotte and Sarrazin generally got on well together, they did have some differences; in spite of Bernadotte's well-known outspokeness the letter may not have been quoted entirely correctly as Sarrazin did not publish it until sixteen years after the event.

Bernadotte spent the autumn and early winter with his troops in Coblenz during which time he was greatly annoyed and upset about an allegation made in one of the Paris newspapers that when in Nuremberg he had plundered the city and accepted bribes from the municipal authorities. It was true that the burgomaster of the city had offered him considerable sums of money and was most surprised when he refused to accept them because, as he told Bernadotte, the Austrian and Prussian generals always accepted similar gifts. Bernadotte, however, told the burgomaster that everyone was master of his own actions and all he wanted, in return for his keeping discipline among his troops, was that proper attention should be paid to the sick and the wounded.

He was so outraged at the allegation made in the Paris newspapers that he wrote to the Directory the following letter which was published in *Le Moniteur* of 10 November 1796:

Coblenz, 7 Brumaire, An 5

'Citizen Directors,

'A certain Duperron has caused to be published in no. 22 of the *Messager du Soir* or *Gazette General de l'Europe* the most revolting calumnies. My regard for my honour compels me to inform you of this fact and to make this complaint to you since owing to your authority you are in a position to make known the truth in the full light of day. This person Duperron alleges that the fine city of Nuremberg was for twenty-four hours given over to plunder, and that General Bernadotte on entering it exacted a contribution within a given number of hours, threatening in default to deliver over the city to the fury of his army. He offers to produce evidence of this. I shall not speak of the indignation shown by the officers and men who know me when they heard of this mendacious assertion ... but I must claim from you the just reparation which is due to me. So infamous a deed cannot remain unpunished and I venture to hope that the Government will explain it in all its heinousness.'

This letter did not at first get much response and the Directory let Bernadotte know that in their opinion he should not take so much notice of something appearing about a well-known general in one of the papers. He was so annoyed with this reaction that he applied to be allowed to retire on half-pay. This request was refused by the Directory but the refusal was conveyed to him in a complimentary letter which once again advised him 'to treat with silent contempt' the unfounded report which had appeared in the Press and also stated that the Directory 'relied on his talents and patriotism to continue ably serving his country'.

But Bernadotte still was not satisfied and probably would have left the army had it not been for Kleber who managed to persuade him to stay put. The advice which Kleber gave his fellow general has been recorded by Sarrazin.

'If you return to France, my dear Bernadotte, with your frank disposition and love of justice, I prophesy that you will perish before three months are over. Not only is the Government composed of five robbers, but every village is governed by a mayor of the same stamp. Like master, like man. The secret police—which is in regard to politics what the science of mining is to the art of war—consists of a set of scoundrels who abuse their power to glut their vengeance, and to cause the most virtuous character to perish or, at least, to suffer disgrace. In vain will you conduct yourself as an honest citizen; they will counterfeit your handwriting; they will accuse you of a traitorous correspondence of which you never had the least idea; and through the perfidy of enemies, whom those envious of your merits will not fail to raise against you, all your fine projects of philosophy and retreat will only tend to cause you to perish on a scaffold as a traitor to your country, as was the case with Custine, Beauharnais and Houchard and many other brave military men. Our governors are lawyers jealous of the glory of their generals; they are base, uninformed, proud, vindictive and cruel—in a word they possess only genius for doing evil. Their dominion cannot last long. Providence always sooner or later does justice on the wicked and recompenses the good. . . . I admit that you might be happy for a month in your rural life, but no sooner would you hear the sound of drums of the National Guard than recollections dear to your heart would make you regret the army. You were born to live in camps and die on the field of battle. . . . You will again wish to hear the acclamations of applause with which your Grenadiers have so often hailed the excellent manœuvres you have caused them to execute on the day of battle. . . . We have for four years fought together in the same ranks. I always felt a brother's tenderness for you; and as a sincere friend I ask you to remain with us.'[1]

It is very doubtful whether he would not have left the army had it not been for the respect and affection which he felt for his brother officer Kleber. On 26 October, just two days before he wrote the letter to the Executive Directory, his sister had died and his mother and elder brother, both of whom still lived in Pau, were the only members of his family left.

As far as his future career was concerned his decision could not have been better, for within two months he was to be sent to reinforce Bonaparte's army in Italy which was to lead to his becoming a Marshal of France and, later on, to a kingdom.

On 20 January 1797 Napoleon had asked the Directory to send him a distinguished divisional commander. 'As to generals of divisons', he wrote, ' I beg of you to send me none but distinguished officers, for our methods of warfare here are so different from all others that I cannot trust a division to any general until I have tried him in two or three engagements.' To this letter he received the following reply: 'The General of Division Bernadotte ... has already won from us proof of your approval and we hope that you will be able to report favourably of his services.'

With a force of about 20,000 Bernadotte marched from his winter quarters in Coblenz to Milan via Metz, Dijon, Lyons, Chambéry and over the Alps by the pass of Mont Cenis to Turin, and eventually Padua—a distance of not less than 600 miles and in the depth of winter.

During this long march Napoleon was negotiating a treaty with the Pope in Tolentino, so was unable to meet his new general and the powerful reinforcements from the Army of the Sambre et Meuse. He did, however, send Bernadotte the following message: 'I greatly desire to make your acquaintance. I am three days away from Rome but we are coming to a treaty with the Pope.'[2]

These two great generals did not actually meet before March and it is unlikely that either of them had any idea of the mixture of antagonism and comradeship which lay before them. Several descriptions of their meeting have been handed down to posterity, the two most reliable ones being probably those given by the two historians Touchard-Lafosse and Leonce Pingaud. According to Lafosse, Bernadotte's account of the meeting was as follows: 'He received me very well but I saw in him a young man of twenty-five or twenty-six, who assumes the airs of a man of fifty, and in my opinion does not bode well for the Republic.' Napoleon apparently criticised Bernadotte's rather swaggering style and later said, according to Pingaud, that 'he possessed a French head and a Roman heart', and 'was a Republican grafted upon a French cavalier'.

There is little doubt that from the time of their first meeting, though they apparently appreciated each other's ability, there was never a feeling of complete trust between them. Of all Bernadotte's friendships and enmities, those with Napoleon were the most important, and lasted for thirteen years, from their first meeting until their last in the summer of 1810 when Napoleon allowed Bernadotte to accept election as the Crown Prince of Sweden. During these eventful years much water was to run under the bridge.

CHAPTER SIX

The Army of Italy

A few weeks after Bernadotte and his troops arrived as much-needed reinforcements to the Army of Italy, the invasion of Austria was about to begin. The strength of the French Army was by then over 60,000 and was spread along a line from the Tyrolean Alps to the shores of the Gulf of Venice. Joubert was in command of the left wing, Massena was in the centre and Napoleon himself took direct command of the right wing in which Bernadotte commanded one of the divisions. Apparently Napoleon was very satisfied with Bernadotte during this operation. Under him was a junior general, General Murat, who later was promoted to Marshal and eventually became King of Naples.[1]

Four months later Bernadotte was to become involved in politics for the first time in his life. This was in connection with two addresses which were sent on Napoleon's orders to the Executive Directory by four of his generals. Under the constitution the two legislative assemblies changed their members by means of the retirement each year of one third of them. It was, therefore, almost certain that as a result of the Reign of Terror this would some day lead to a constitutional crisis, for there were many who, although they wished France to remain a republic, did not approve of much that had happened since 1793, and quite a number who would like to see the restoration of the monarchy.

After the May election of 1797 the Council had to elect

a president, and two candidates were put up: Jourdan, who was a firm Republican and in favour of maintaining the present constitution, and General Pichegru, who was a Royalist.

When the poll was held Pichegru was elected by a large majority. Briefly, when this was known, Bonaparte arranged for four extremely anti-royalist addresses to be written and signed by the four generals in question: Massena, Serrurier, Joubert and Augereu. They were sent, not directly to the Executive Directory, but forwarded through him.

Napoleon wanted Bernadotte to do the same but he would have none of it. He told his Commander-in-Chief quite bluntly that he considered that instructions given to the other generals were most unwise and an infraction of the constitution, and that neither Napoleon nor any other Commander-in-Chief had the authority to order a subordinate commander to send such a letter. Having, therefore, made his position crystal clear he wrote the following letter and sent it direct to the Executive Directory with a copy to Napoleon.

'To the Executive Directory

'Rumours of counter-revolution are heard on all sides to which the men whom I command refuse to give the slightest credence; but, if they turn out to be true, if the conspirators have planned to lay a sacrilegious hand on the Government which is the safeguard of the laws and the sentinel of the people, then be assured that there still exist the arms which have served the cause of national independence and the Chiefs who have led the phalanxes of the Republic. With such supports as these you have only to express the wish in order that the enemies of the State and of liberty may disappear.

J.-B. Bernadotte'

The contents of this letter must either have been made public or reached the press by a leak because a newspaper named *Le Grondeur*, whose policy was slightly to the right of centre, commented on it and claimed that General Bernadotte was in sympathy with their point of view. He replied with a letter which made it clear that he was Republican 'both by principle and conviction', and that as his 'life had always been dedicated to military labours' he had to submit to the duties of his station, which meant that if at any time either the government or the Republic were in danger he would feel it necessary to defend them and call to his assistance the brave men who had so often heard his voice in the field of glory. The letter led Albert Sorel to ask the question whether it did not demonstrate that in Bernadotte's mind there were 'latent instincts of kingship'.[2]

Very shortly after, Bernadotte was ordered by Napoleon to go to Paris to hand over to the Directory a number of captured Austrian regimental colours. In a letter which Bernadotte was given to present to the Directory Napoleon paid him many compliments; he wrote:

> 'That excellent general who has made his reputation on the banks of the Rhine is today one of the officers who are most necessary to the glory of the Army of Italy. I cannot allow this opportunity to pass of expressing the tribute of praise which I owe to the services of his brave division.... You see in General Bernadotte one of the most foremost friends of the Republic, incapable alike by his principles and character of sacrificing the cause of liberty or the obligations of honour.'

Bernadotte had not been in Paris long before he wrote a letter to Napoleon saying how much he disliked it. 'Paris is a horrible place for a man of honour', he wrote, 'and I am already wearied to death with it.' His mission to Paris, however, seems to have puzzled the new Governor and Commander-in-Chief of the garrison, General Augereau, one of Napoleon's generals who had obeyed his orders to write a violently anti-royalist letter to the Directory. Augereau thought that Bernadotte's visit was unnecessary and he even went so far as to write to Napoleon to tell him that Bernadotte 'had been received with demonstrations of surprise and fear'.

At the end of the formal ceremony at which the colours were presented on behalf of the Army of Italy to the Directory, the President Larevellière-Lépaux expressed their gratitude to 'Bernadotte's intrepid comrades and himself', and then gave Bernadotte an affectionate embrace which caused him great embarrassment because the President was a regicide and a real revolutionary of the Reign of Terror.

Before Bernadotte was due to leave Paris, however, the coup d'état of 18 Fructidor (4 September) took place. It is evident from the contents of a letter which he wrote to Napoleon on 15 Fructidor that he had a strong suspicion that something was going to happen before very long.

> 'The Royalist party has changed its tactics. It no longer dares to tilt against the Directory. Yet in my opinion it should be pursued and denounced, in order that the patriots may be able to direct public opinion on wise and prudent lines and thus ensure the results of the coming elections. But in order to succeed in that task wisdom and prudence are necessary.
>
> 'Any violent and ill-directed movement must necessarily be fatal to liberty, because the abuses of power always increase when the will of individuals is substituted for the law of the land. We are in danger of being obliged to invest

> the Depositories of the law with a consular power and to declare the temporary suspension of the two other authorities of the state.... At present the Republic seems like a young colt which prances and bounds after having been kept too long in the stable.'

The most interesting part of the letter is the forecast of the probable necessity for empowering a consul to lead the state because just over a year later, after the Brumaire coup d'état, the Directory was superseded by Napoleon as First Consul. It was, no doubt, the coup d'état of 18 Fructidor, by setting a precedent, which paved the way for his own coup, and the fact that the Royalists were kept out left an obvious way open for Napoleon.

Bernadotte did not return to Italy until a month after the Fructidor coup d'état. He only did so because he turned down the offer of Commander-in-Chief of the Southern Army which consisted of four divisions stationed in the region of Marseilles which was still in a turbulent state.

In a letter which he wrote to Barras, one of the leading members of the Executive Directory, he gave his reason for turning down the offer.

> 'I have accordingly searched my conscience and have carefully considered the duties which it would involve and the means necessary for fulfilment and I dare not accept an employment requiring a profound knowledge, a close study of human nature and a character at once firm and conciliatory. My honour, the voice of my conscience and my desire to be useful to my country bid me to refuse the offer. Do not inist on converting a good soldier into a bad chief.'

On the same day he wrote to Napoleon telling him that there was a rumour going about that Napoleon intended to disband his (Bernadotte's) division and form a new one out of it. Bernadotte said that he refused to believe it because Napoleon had promised him before his departure from Milan that the division would be retained for him until he returned from Paris. 'Besides you know, my General,' he wrote, 'that my division is my military family and I am attached to it.' He also told Napoleon that he had just refused a command consisting of four divisions and that he would arrive in Italy about the same time as his letter, namely in eleven days.

When Bernadotte eventually did return to Italy, which was later than the proposed eleven days, he saw Napoleon at Undine, near the Austrian frontier. The first thing Napoleon did was to ask him what the Directory's views were about the impending negotiations with the Austrians; in Paris the Directory had said that on no account should Venice be ceded to Austria. Finally Napoleon asked what the Directory thought about himself. Bernadotte's reply has been recorded in Sarrazin's *Biographical Sketch*:

> 'The Directory is annoyed at the want of respect which you give to them' [Bernadotte is supposed to have said] 'the Army of the Sambre et Meuse is opposed to you and the Army of the Rhine believes you to be the cause of Moreau's disgrace. The Royalists know that the events of Fructidor have put a stop to their plans and that one of the objects of the coup d'état was to save you from the charges which they wished to bring against you. The Republicans suspect you and have been cool even about your fame. The people of Paris, however, are enthusiastic about you. The blood that was shed on 13 Vendiaire is washed away from the walls. You are today the idol of the populace who would on that occasion have willingly seen you carried to the guillotine.'

What Napoleon's reaction was to Bernadotte's account of his popularity has never been recorded but it had ended quite complimentarily and it is not improbable that Napoleon preferred to be the idol of the populace than of anyone else.

Before October was out the first serious rift took place between these two very different personalities. Bernadotte received orders from Napoleon to break up his division and hand over part of it to another general, in spite of the assurances previously given. This was a great blow to him; he felt that he had been let down by someone who had always spoken highly of him.

On 28 November he applied to the Directory asking for some other command; failing that, he wanted to retire from the service. Simultaneously he sent the following letter to his Commander-in-Chief:

> 'I send you, General, a copy of a request I have made to the Directory. If my retirement is granted me, I beg you will employ in the Army of England the citizens Villate and Maurin my aides-de-camp. They are good subjects. They will serve the Republic with the same zeal and ardour which have always characterised the troops from the Rhine. They will, like me, bow to superior talents but never to mere audacity. Although I have grounds for complaint against you I shall part from you without ceasing to have for your talents my greatest esteem.'

There is one thing about the subject of this book which should be evident by now, namely that whether he was engaged in conversation or correspondence with someone, Bernadotte usually gave as good as he got.

Napoleon's reply demonstrates that although he did not and never did really like Bernadotte he did not want, if it could be avoided, to become his enemy.

'I have received, Citizen General, your last letter. The Executive Directory assure me that they will be eager to do all they can to please you. They have decided to give you the choice of the command of the Ionian Isles or of a division in the Army of England which will be augmented by the addition of your old troops of the Army of the Sambre et Meuse.... No one appreciates more than I do the purity of your principles, the loyalty of your character, and the military talents which you have developed while we have served together. You will do me an injustice if you doubt it for a moment. In all circumstances I shall count on your esteem and friendship.... I salute you.

Bonaparte'

Very shortly after this was written Napoleon received a letter from the Directory that they wanted Bernadotte to take over command of the Army of Italy. Napoleon wrote and congratulated Bernadotte, but under the counter he did everything he could to get the Directory to cancel the offer, explaining that Bernadotte was a very ordinary soldier who had been for many years in the ranks and possessed only 'limited intellectual capabilities'. He succeeded in getting the government to appoint Bernadotte as ambassador to Austria. The appointment only lasted for five months and Bernadotte did not like it at all.

CHAPTER SEVEN

Ambassador to Austria

It was, in any event, strange, after all that had happened since the Revolution and the Reign of Terror began, that the French Republic should send an ambassador to Vienna. Only five years had elapsed since Marie Antoinette, Archduchesse d'Autriche, had been guillotined and ever since then both countries had been constantly at war with each other. Many distinguished aristocrats had emigrated to Austria and had been granted refuge there.

The main reason for Bernadotte's disliking this new appointment he gave in correspondence with the Directory and Talleyrand, the French Foreign Minister. 'The first quality of a soldier, which is obedience,' he wrote in his letter to the Directory in which he accepted the appointment, 'forbids me to hesitate; but I fear that I shall meet greater difficulties in diplomacy than any which I have had to overcome in my military career.'[1]

To Talleyrand he wrote several letters including the following, dated 28 January 1798.

> 'In accepting the important mission which the Government have just confided to me I have consulted my capacity less than my desire to be useful to the Republic. I have said to myself that in a young republic the men who cherish the love of serving her should approach high office as they approach death—neither desiring it nor fearing it.

I confess, and do so without a blush, that although the events of my life, which have so rapidly succeeded each other, have been such as to fortify the courage of my soul, that courage which has served me in my military career would now have abandoned me, and I should, in spite of my unalterable wish to sacrifice my tranquility on the altar of my country, have shrunk from so difficult a task, if the hope of being aided by your counsel had not set my mind at ease. I place boundless reliance upon your willingness to advise me, because I believe that you have contributed to my appointment.'[2]

The government did all they could to make Bernadotte feel more resigned to the new appointment including the grant of a salary of 140,000 francs, plus allowances for travelling, etc. He also had some difficulty in choosing his own staff, which he very much wanted to do. He argued that although he had just been appointed ambassador he still held the rank of general, and was, therefore, entitled to keep his two aides-de-camp, Captains Maurin and Villate.

Eventually he wrote a letter to Barras because he had been experiencing much opposition on this subject from Talleyrand. Finally under pressure from the Directory he gave way. The job which he was now facing he knew to be difficult, particularly for the reason already given above, but in some ways he was the best man to have been chosen, because, due to his fairness when in occupation of certain parts of the country with his troops, he had earned a good reputation in the eyes of many of the Austrian authorities and certainly a much better one than had a number of other French generals.

The Austrian Foreign Minister himself opposed the appointment of a French ambassador but it was not

Bernadotte to whom he objected. The Austrian attitude was that this was an inopportune time for the appointment of any French ambassador and that before it had been made there should have been some negotiations.

The Austrian Foreign Minister's opposition did not succeed and on 8 February Bernadotte arrived in Vienna. Following the usual protocol he had an audience with the Emperor which apparently went very well.

> 'The peace signed at Campo Formio between the French Republic and your Imperial Majesty' [Bernadotte told the Emperor] 'has caused the Directory to entrust me with the post of ambassador to your Majesty. In accepting that honourable and important mission I have yielded to the desire to contribute to a friendship and a just understanding between the Powers, who in critical times have measured each other's strength and have learned the lesson of mutual respect. It will be my principal object to convince your Majesty that the Directory of the French Republic is sincerely attached to its friends and that it gives unqualified support and protection to its allies. I shall be doubly happy if I can convince your Majesty of the sincerity of my wishes that your Majesty may enjoy peace and happiness.'

Anyone who realised the real animosity between the Austrians and the French could not have helped foreseeing that it would not be long before something would happen in Vienna. On the afternoon of 13 April a very large tricolour flag was hoisted over the French embassy. This had been done because of complaints from the Directory that there had been 'no display of the national colours'.[3] It happened to be Easter week and the youth of Vienna had organised a demonstration to celebrate the first anniversary of Austrian volunteers having enlisted for the defence of Vienna against the French army, in which at that time Bernadotte had been serving as a general. The demonstrators were marching through the streets and, quite naturally, included the French embassy on their route. Outside the crowd gathered shouting anti-French slogans and throwing stones through the windows. Bernadotte, as was his nature, went to the porch of the embassy and tried to address the crowd. It was so noisy, however, that he could not make himself heard. One of the crowd climbed the balcony, tore down the flag and then burned it. The ashes were then taken by the demonstrators to the imperial palace. What happened after that has been described by Frederic Masson in *Les Diplomates de la Revolution.* According to him the crowd after burning the flag broke into the Lichtenstein Palace 'and having sacked the ground floor proceeded to mount the stairs. Here they were met by the ambassador and his staff who stood at the head of the staircase with drawn swords and warned the people that they would sell their lives dearly.... Eventually about one o'clock a squadron of cuirassiers arrived and dispersed the rioters.'[4]

Bernadotte had protested to the Austrian Foreign Minister before the riots finally ended, but as all the replies which he received to these and subsequent protests were, in his opinion, unsatisfactory he sent a letter to the Emperor written formally in the third person demanding his passports.

> 'In leaving Vienna he will carry away the consoling consciousness of having left nothing undone to convince His Imperial Majesty of the peaceful and friendly disposition which the French government entertain for him. He also rejoices in the belief that His Majesty is profoundly grieved at the attack directed against the representative of a friendly Power, and that all the measures which propriety demanded would have been taken if His Majesty's

intentions had been faithfully fulfilled. The Ambassador hopes that the future will confirm his opinion in some striking manner, and that a just reparation will prove to the Executive Directory that His Imperial Majesty is no less desirous than they are for the maintenance of good understanding between the two nations.'[5]

In a reply the Emperor hoped that Bernadotte would not leave. He also promised to initiate a full inquiry into the demonstration and expressed his wish, as Bernadotte had mentioned in his letter, for good relations between their two countries. After writing in reply to the Emperor's letter that he was not prepared to remain in Vienna as French ambassador Bernadotte left on 15 April.

The next few days were most unpleasant for him. When he reached Rastadt on the 23 April he wrote to the Directory demanding that they should issue some statement justifying his conduct and officially recalling him to Paris, which they had not yet done. The next few weeks were spent by the Directory trying to make up their minds what their final reaction should be to the Vienna affair. There was trouble between Napoleon and Barras. The former said that the whole trouble occurred due to Bernadotte's imprudence, hot-headedness and failure to understand the point of view of the Viennese.

Barras reminded Napoleon, however, that it was he and no one else who had deprived Bernadotte of his command of the Army of Italy and had suggested that he should be given the appointment of ambassador to Vienna.[6]

To get rid of Napoleon, at least temporarily, the Directory sent him to Egypt and he had already been at sea for a few days when they changed their minds slightly and offered Bernadotte the appointment of ambassador to the Batavian Republic. Whether this offer was a serious one seems unlikely because they already knew that he had never wanted to go to Vienna and that it was most improbable, particularly having regard to the unpleasant incident which had just taken place, that he would accept any other diplomatic appointment.

His letter refusing the offer gave his reasons quite clearly and also provided him with the opportunity of giving his own views about the incident that had caused all this trouble. This letter was published in *Le Moniteur* on 1 June 1798.

'Citizen Directors,

'The Minister of Foreign Relations [Talleyrand] has informed me that you have nominated me Minister Plenipotentiary to the Batavian Republic. The offer of such an honourable employment cannot but afford gratification ... but you have already been made acquainted with my wishes and my disinclination for the diplomatic career.... You know that the Embassy to the Imperial Court was not wished for by me, and that my acceptance of it was intended by me as an act of obedience and as a fresh mark of devotion to the Republic.... I receive with respect your approbation of my military and diplomatic conduct. All that concerns my diplomatic career has a certain interest for me on account of the errors into which several newspapers have fallen, in the accounts which they have given to the public. It gives me great pleasure to think that the time is not far distant when the policy of the Government will permit them to inform the French people of the exact truth. I beg you, Citizen Directors, to receive the tribute of my gratitude. You have rightly felt that the reputation of a man, who had contributed to place upon its pedestal the statue of liberty, was a national property.'

One of the accounts 'given to the public' by the newspaper which, not surprisingly, had annoyed him, had described him as 'the man of Vienna with the little flag'.

Even in England the press made much of the incident. In October there was an article in *The Times*, under the heading of 'Peace', in which the following paragraph appeared. 'What would a peace avail us which would grant protection for other Bernadottes to come to this country and diffuse among us the seeds of a new revolution as the French ambassadors have done in Spain and other countries?'

CHAPTER EIGHT

A Memory of the Past

When Bernadotte was twenty-seven years old and serving in a battalion of the Regiment Royal-la-Marine, whose colonel was Marquis d'Ambert, an incident took place which was described in detail in another chapter. On that occasion the Marquis was saved from the fury of a revolutionary mob in Marseilles by the bravery of Bernadotte, and very shortly after this, knowing that the attack had been made on him because he was an aristocrat, d'Ambert resigned from the army and left France. His name in accordance with the regulations in force at that time, was put on the list of emigrés.

It so happened that at the time of the coup d'état of the 18 Fructidor a law was passed under which anyone on the emigré list who was found in France could be brought before a Military Commission and sentenced to death. Although d'Ambert had not emigrated from France in the real sense of the word—for he always intended to come back and in fact did so after an absence of less than eight months—someone decided to put this law into operation against him. It would probably have been much wiser if d'Ambert had done nothing and merely laid low. Although there had been a warrant issued for his arrest, seven months had elapsed and no apparent steps had been taken to bring him to 'justice', if such a word may be used in this context. Unfortunately, remembering how Bernadotte had protected him eight years ago when he was only an NCO, d'Ambert quite naturally thought that now Bernadotte was a general he would have a much better chance of helping him.

Bernadotte had only recently been sent to Vienna as the French ambassador and had been since then very much in the public eye, so d'Ambert wrote a letter which was published in the *Amis des Lois* on 1 March 1798. In it he mentioned that the popular Republican General Bernadotte had in fact been promoted by him to the rank of Adjutant. ... 'His good fortune gives me some consolation for the unmerited persecution to which I have been subjected for the last month ...'

The unfortunate result of the publication of this letter was that all the necessary steps were immediately taken to arrest him and bring him before the Military Commission, who ordered him to be shot. A petition was presented to the Council of Five Hundred asking for a reprieve and suggesting that the case should be brought before a committee for reconsideration. This was done, but from the report of it which was published in *Le Moniteur* there is no doubt that even getting rid of Robespierre and the other regicides had made little difference in the Terror which still took the place of justice in the French Republic. One deputy supported the petition but the remainder did not even bother to consider the facts and merits of d'Ambert's case.

Bernadotte who, of course, had heard about the so-called trial of his former colonel went to see the Directory and asked them to reprieve him. His request met with no success. What actually happened is to be found in Barras' memoirs.[1]

> 'After having revealed, perhaps somewhat severely, the weak side of Bernadotte as a public man I should consider myself worthy of censure, were I to overlook traits which reflect credit on the private individual.

'Bernadotte had heard of the arrest of the colonel of his old regiment of Royal-la-Marine in which he had served as a private and a sergeant: this was the Marquis d'Ambert who, proscribed pursuant to the law against emigrés, had been recognised while strolling about Paris, arrested and turned over to the Military Commission. It was on this occasion that Bernadotte's sincere and generous soul stood revealed to us. He promptly called on the Directory to beg that his former colonel's offence might be condoned. "It is," he said, "the only price I ask for my services". Bernadotte had, on a former occasion, at the time of a riot in Marseilles, saved the life of the Marquis d'Ambert; in those days he was nothing more than a sergeant. Bernadotte, who had in the meantime become a general, was not to be so successful on this occasion. He had to deal with a Director, Merlin, a former Minister of Justice, a man far more terrible than the popular fury of the early days of the Revolution. I moved that the Marquis d'Ambert be conducted to the frontier. Merlin called for his execution, which took place.'

CHAPTER NINE

His Meeting with Désirée Clary

When the Viennese affair was all over, bar a few comments which continued to be made for some time by those who disliked Bernadotte, he was able to have a few months of the summer of 1798 in Paris and, practically for the first time in his life, meet some of those who now formed the new Parisian society. It was in this way that he came to meet his future wife, Désirée Clary.

Both of Napoleon's brothers, Joseph and Lucien, were members of the Council of Five Hundred and it was in Joseph's house that he first met her. In the early 1790s Joseph had wanted to marry her but Napoleon had stepped in, told his brother that Julie, Désirée's elder sister, would make a better wife for him and that he wanted to marry Désirée.[1]

From then until he met Josephine de Beauharnais, Napoleon and his chosen one carried on as though they were one day going to get married, although there appears to be no real evidence that they were ever officially engaged. Very shortly after his first meeting with Josephine the attachment came to an end. For some time afterwards Désirée went to live in Rome with her sister Julie and her brother-in-law Joseph who was by then the French ambassador there. She became engaged to General Duphot, an engagement which came to a tragic end; a riot took place outside the French embassy and in the disturbance Duphot was killed.

It was after Joseph left Rome and returned to Paris that

Bernadotte became a close friend of the family and met Désirée. Even between her arrival with her brother-in-law and her meeting with Bernadotte, Désirée had had other suitors including Junot, who later became the Duc d'Abrantes, and Marmont, who later became a marshal and a duke. It was this past history of Désirée which led a French writer, M. Houssage, to write of her:

> 'Désirée Clary was intended for earthly honours, and at least they rested lightly on her head. Let us recapitulate. She is betrothed to Joseph, then to Napoleon, then to Junot and would be glad to accept Marmont; at last she marries Bernadotte. With Joseph she would have been an Imperial Princess, Queen of Naples and of Spain; with Napoleon Empress of the French; with Duphot probably Maréchale and Duchesse; with Junot, Duchesse d'Abrantes; with Marmont, Maréchale and Duchess of Ragusa. Bernadotte, the former sergeant of marines, placed the crown of Sweden on the head of this little bourgeoise of Marseilles.'

Bernadotte was well up to the standard of the many other distinguished suitors, even though nobody guessed that he would one day be elected to the throne of Sweden and found the Bernadotte dynasty. He had many attractive characteristics, described by a number of people who obviously meant what they said. Perhaps the greatest was a charm of manner.

The Comte de Rochechouart, a French aristocrat who had emigrated to Russia and became ADC to the Emperor, wrote this about him:

> 'He was tall and slight; his eagle countenance was exactly like that of the great Condé; his thick black hair harmonised with the colourless complexion of the inhabitants

of Bearn, his native province. His appearance on horseback was very martial, perhaps a little theatrical, but his daring and coolness in the bloodiest of battles made one willing to forget this defect. It is impossible to meet a man of more seductive manners and conversation. He captivated me entirely and if I had been attached to his person I should have been entirely devoted to him.'

General Zurlinden, who after he ceased to be a soldier became a writer, described Bernadotte as 'tall, well-built with a handsome appearance. His eyes were bright and piercing. His features were energetic, clear cut, in the style of Condé. He worked hard, was eloquent and a leader of men.'

The final compliment which he could be paid came from the King and Queen of Sweden by whom he was adopted shortly after his election as Prince of Sweden. They both adored him as though he were their own son, and even the Queen Mother said that he was a 'most lovable person'. No doubt all these characteristics and his charm were greatly appreciated by Désirée herself, but she once said that another reason why she so quickly took to him was that he was a man who could stand up to Napoleon. 'Il est un homme,' someone told her, 'a tenir tête à Napoléon.'

Although he was fond of her the marriage presented difficulties for him; the rest of the Bonaparte family liked him very much and it was not, therefore, always so easy to resist and disagree with Napoleon when he thought it necessary, which he frequently did. Nevertheless it also had an advantage, because there were occasions when he escaped a showdown with Napoleon because Désirée was his wife. Many years later, when he was a prisoner on St Helena, Napoleon said on three occasions that he would have had Bernadotte shot had it not been for Désirée.

CHAPTER TEN

Minister of War

Bernadotte commanded the left wing of the Army of the Mainz from October 1798 until January 1799. The Directory then offered him the command of the Army of Italy, but he refused it because they could not give him the number of troops which he considered necessary. It was then accepted by General Schérer, the Minister for War, with the tragic result that in less than two months he was defeated at the battle of Magnano and France lost all her conquests in Italy. Bernadotte, who had more or less predicted this, had been quite right. Even Barras himself, who was sometimes critical of Bernadotte, on this occasion agreed with his forecast. It appears in his memoirs that the conditions which Bernadotte laid down as a condition for his accepting the command 'were justified by events, and that his advice to the Government turned out to have been well-informed and sound'.

During April and May of 1799 Bernadotte was away on sick-leave, but returned to Paris at the end of May. During his absence an important change had taken place in the Directory; one of the members named Rewbell had been replaced by Sieyès who was the French ambassador in Berlin. Apart from Barras, Sieyès' four colleagues were not of great standing and he and Barras decided to get rid of them. This decision led up to what was known as the coup d'état of 30 Prairial which fortunately was successful without any troops being involved.

Once the new Directory had been formed it became necessary to form a new government, in which Bernadotte became Minister of War. The only person who objected to his appointment was Sieyès whom André Maurois has described as 'a soured clergyman with a cold moderate outlook'.[1] Sieyès gave his reason for opposing the appointment of Bernadotte. It was because he did not approve of having a soldier as Minister of War. It was widely known, however, that Sieyès had a personal dislike of Bernadotte. His appointment only lasted from 2 July to 14 September 1799 but a great deal was to happen during those ten weeks, in which he did much to restore the spirit of the army which had been deteriorating.

It was Director Barras who actually proposed at a meeting of the Directory Council the appointment of Bernadotte. 'We want,' he said, 'a man esteemed for his achievements and for his character.... I propose Bernadotte as Minister of War.'

A very good and detailed description of Bernadotte's daily work as Minister of War is to be found in Barras' memoirs. It is certainly a responsible and accurate account because the editor of his memoirs was actually Secretary of the War Department under Bernadotte.

> 'Bernadotte, who lived in the rue Cisalpine at the extremity of the Faubourg de Roule, did not take up his residence at the Ministry, but continued to reside at his home, which was a maisonette that hardly cost 20,000 francs. But he was attached to it because he had purchased it with his military savings ... and because it was there that his wife had just given birth to a son, the only one they ever had, who is now Crown Prince and heir presumptive to the throne of Sweden. Continuing to sleep at his home he rose

every day at 3 a.m. and arrived at the Ministry at 4 a.m. with his secretary for whom he called on his way. His aides-de-camp were utilised for administrative work.

When he had first been appointed he had given orders at the Ministry that nothing should remain for more than twenty-four hours undisposed of, or, at all events un-considered and unanswered, and he had infused such energy into the Department that this order, which appeared at first hardly possible of execution, was rigorously carried out and everything was up-to-date. In this way, he said in his proclamations, he had to reorganise and create every-thing, to raise a hundred battalions of a thousand men each, forty thousand cavalry, etc.... each day he worked in his office fifteen or sixteen hours a day. Bernadotte himself sent letters to all the Generals of Division trying to boost their morale which was, not surprisingly, low because of the lack of organisation of supplies, arms, and ammuni-tion.'

The letter set out below was dispatched six days after he had become Minister.

'To the Generals of Division:

'The Directory has just confided to me the Department of War. If, at the moment of national danger, it were allowable to consult my own preferences, you will be right in believing that I would have refused the Ministry and already rejoined my comrades at the front. But in view of the ruinous condition of every branch of military ad-ministration I have felt that the very difficulty of the enter-prise imposed on me the obligation to accept. My vigils are entirely devoted to the task of relieving the necessities of my brothers-in-arms.... I have seen those glorious days when the generals did their duty six times over on the field of battle and the promotion which was conferred upon us was the reward of those extraordinary exertions. It is by the same virtues and the same energy that liberty is to be reconquered. To win success you have only got to recall your past achievements.... At your voice there will issue from the ranks those children of Liberty who are bound to be her preservers. Spare no pains in seeking them out. Lose no time in pointing them out to me. They shall be promptly promoted. They are the men who will conquer Europe.'

Another much-needed step was taken by the new minister. A number of generals who had been got rid of by his predecessor, because they were suspected of not being revolutionary enough, were reinstated and given commands. It is not unusual for any Minister of War to have some difficulty in obtaining enough money from the Treasury for defence purposes and Bernadotte was no exception. The Republic's funds were at their lowest and it was not easy for France, the enemy of practically every country in Europe, to obtain any international credit.

The Minister of Finance was also a newcomer, but Bernadotte did not find him easy to deal with and it certainly did not work when he started riding the high horse as was his wont. Lindet—for that was the minister's name—eventually, with the help of the heads of his other departments, managed to convince Bernadotte that there were no funds available in the national treasury. Early in August, however, some Genoese bankers lent the government money and Bernadotte was then able to fulfil part of his promise to send some of it to the Army of Italy, which was then commanded by Joubert, and needed it most.

It was not long after this, while Bernadotte was still

Minister, that Joubert was killed in the battle of Novi. He was only thirty years old and would, doubtless, have had a brilliant career because to be a Commander-in-Chief at so young an age was unusual. Bernadotte sent a special message to the Army of Italy which did much to counteract the depression which Joubert's death had caused, not only in the army but also in government circles.

'To the Army of Italy,

'For three years Joubert remained unknown and unrecognised in the obscure ranks of the army; and now his death has riveted the respectful attention of Europe. What is the secret of so great a reputation? Soldiers of the fatherland, this is another of Liberty's miracles. She raises to the sky her generous defenders.... He has perished in your midst in the flower of his age. As he fell from his horse, he exclaimed to you with his last breath, "Forward my comrades. Forward." You heard his dying words. You have sworn on his tomb to avenge him. Your tears will have not been in vain.... Rally round that eternal principle of victory—discipline. It will bring back to you the success which is only delayed. Numerous reinforcements representing every arm of the service are on their way to support you. Let the old soldiers give to the young conscripts the example of order and of duty.... Brave friends, the stock of brave generals is not exhausted. When we lived under kings, it was possible for men to say that nature requires repose after having produced a great man. But I see among you more than one Joubert, more than one Bonaparte. Liberty has transformed nature.

Bernadotte'

This address, which was also published in *Le Moniteur* on 30 August 1799, could certainly be described as one of

Bernadotte's well-known 'gasconnades'. It also seems to have been written in such a way as to please both ardent revolutionaries and moderate republicans. It seems somewhat strange that Napoleon is said to have been pleased with the reference to himself, for many people were of the opinion that in Napoleon's eyes he was the only Bonaparte.

A general who had just as good an opinion of himself as did Napoleon was Massena who, while Bernadotte was Minister of War, was in command of the Army of the Danube. He had never got on well with Bernadotte and objected to his interference with his plans for an operation in August 1799, the details of which are not important. Massena had refused to carry out certain orders which Bernadotte had issued with the sanction of the Directory. Bernadotte accordingly sent him the following despatch: 'You must not delay an instant in carrying out the wishes of the Directory. The first and last virtue is obedience. I cannot too emphatically repeat that if you have not the intention of fighting the battle which France expects and the Directory desires, you are to order, on receipt of this letter, the departure of the 18,000 men.'

Massena's immediate reaction was to ask for permission to resign his command because of ill health and suggest that his successor should at once be appointed. This resulted in another letter from the minister to the recalcitrant general. 'You will have perceived,' wrote Bernadotte, 'by my letter of yesterday that the sending of troops to the Rhine, which you were to have carried out, has been postponed. . . . I know well enough, Citizen General, your devotion to the Republic to believe that you have now forgotten your state of health, and that you have no other wish than to justify the hope of the fatherland in this important crisis.'

This letter was written on the 26 August but as nothing

had apparently happened by 5 September Bernadotte wrote yet one more letter, and did not mince his words. He ended by stating bluntly that as Minister of War it was his duty to invite him, Massena, to realise that the orders of the Directory did not admit delay. It worked, but it is not surprising that Massena's aide-de-camp, who wrote his general's biography, stated that although Bernadotte was 'brave and skilful on the field of battle he did not possess the powerful breadth of vision and wealth of combinations demanded by a vast chess-board'.

There have been many governments in many countries and in many centuries, not excluding the present one, where there has been corruption. Many ministers and politicians have been tempted to accept bribes but, although there are many who have succumbed to the temptation, there has also been a not inconsiderable number who rejected it. In using the word bribes it does not necessarily mean that sums of money were offered.

Bernadotte, while he was Minister of War, was offered rich rewards by all the parties in the new Republic of France but he refused them all. A man named Chiappe tried to get him to bring back the Bourbon monarchy, and suggested that the Duc d'Enghien would be prepared to support Bernadotte in any attempt to restore it and that he, Bernadotte, could be appointed Constable of France (which in the time of the Bourbon dynasty was a very powerful and important post). The Duc d'Enghien, who was Lieutenant-General of the royalist army, was supposed to be in Paris and Bernadotte used this information to his advantage when he wrote to Chiappe about the offer.[2]

> 'The Duc d'Enghien will have no reason to regret the esteem he has exhibited for me. But how could he suppose

that the loyalty of character which he attributes to me could allow me to listen to his proposals? He speaks to me a different language and tells me that, as a Minister of the French Republic, I can have no relation with Royalists except to oppose them.... For seven years France has been a republic, and, as in duty bound, I have taken the oath to obey its laws. My heart repels falsehood, and is devoted to the maintenance of the Constitution and the glory of my country.... That was my rule of conduct under the old monarchical government; that will always be my rule of conduct under the republican regime. Take back this answer to him who sent you, and say that it is sincere and unalterable.... Add that for three days I shall keep the secret which you have communicated to me. That will enable him to cross the frontier, but on the morning of the fourth day I shall inform the Directory of all that has taken place. In the meantime, as this secret might reach the Directory through some other channel, I shall watch the departure of couriers and telegraphic despatches, and protect the escape of the Prince.... Bestir yourself in this matter, and recollect that the least indiscretion may be fatal to yourself.'

The next person to approach Bernadotte was General Jourdan on behalf of the Jacobins, and the minister must have been very interested because the proposition concerned Sieyès, the 'sour clergyman' who tried to prevent Bernadotte from being appointed Minister of War. The Jacobins wanted to get rid of both Sieyès and Barras and in return for Bernadotte's help they were prepared to offer him an important post in the government. He listened to the delegation who came to put the proposal to him but refused to take any part in the scheme. He was not prepared, he told them, while he held the appointment of minister, to become involved in anything unconstitutional. He apparently told them, however, that when he ceased to hold the appointment—and he must have known it would not be long before that happened—he might take a different view.

General Jourdan described this in *Notice sur le Dix-huit Brumaire*: 'I ought to relate, in a reference to this subject,' he wrote, 'a characteristic trait of Bernadotte, which shows his loyalty of character. Having been consulted by me on behalf of my friends he declared that he was ready to take a place in our ranks, and to use his influence over the troops but that before doing anything he would have to give up his portfolio, not wishing to abuse the confidence of the Directory for the purpose of overthrowing it.'

The minister's last temptation was, strangely enough, from Sieyès himself, who asked Bernadotte what he thought about the Directory's recalling Napoleon from Egypt. Napoleon's brothers Joseph and Lucien, appeared to know, or pretended to know, that Barras much wanted him to come back. There is little doubt that both the brothers and Sieyès wanted to change the constitution—which actually happened, as it turned out, about two months later. Once again, however, Bernadotte was not prepared to join in anything before he either resigned or was dismissed from his present appointment.

It was not to be long before that happened, for in that same month Sieyès, speaking of Bernadotte, said: 'We are no longer of any account. Nobody takes any notice of us. It is the Minister of War who constitutes the government.'

Whether or not it was in reply to Sieyès' remark is not known but it was in the same month, September, that Bernadotte said to him 'It has been made clear to me that you are all ice, when you ought to be all fire.'

Having from the start always been against Bernadotte becoming Minister of War, Sieyès, during the nine weeks during which Bernadotte held that office, had grown to dislike him more and more. The reason was because, even in that short time, he had done a great deal to improve the state of the armies, and as a result had become extremely popular not only in the service but in government circles. One of his greatest successes had been in increasing conscription and also having made the conscripts happy that they had joined the army. This was a great achievement on his part because for the past five or six years the public spirit had been getting lower and lower; many young men tried to evade the call-up and many who were called up quite soon afterwards deserted.

As usual he succeeded by appealing to them in his accustomed manner. One of his addresses to the conscripts is set out below:

> 'Young Conscripts,
>
> 'The moment approaches when you are to muster. The law summons you to the standards. A few days ago I reminded your chiefs of their duties.* Today I come to speak to you of yours.... If order is necessary in social life the necessity is more rigorous in military life. The military career has its pains and fatigues, but it has pleasures which surpass them.... The soldier of Liberty takes up arms only to defend his rights. ... Think of the mightiness of France in the days of her slavery. How mighty shall she be now that she has become free!
>
> The Minister of War, Bernadotte.'[3]

Sieyès' reaction to the advice given by Bernadotte to the conscripts has already been mentioned. Barras was not of the

* This was a reference to the address referred to above which he dispatched to Generals of Divisions.

same opinion. He admitted, however, that by his vigorous action Bernadotte was actually governing more than the government was, and he paid him the compliment of saying that he constituted the only military, patriotic and administrative bond which prevented at this moment the breaking up of the Republic. He also said that Bernadotte was as simple-minded and loyal as he was energetic and that everything he did while he was Minister was for the benefit and defence of the Republic.

Sieyès was determined, however, to do everything he could to change the Minister of War, but he found it difficult to get a majority of the Directory to agree to his dismissal and no one at first seemed anxious to take over the ministry from Bernadotte. Later he persuaded Barras to come over to his side and then won over another member, which gave him a majority.

Next day, 28 Fructidor, Sieyès, who was then President of the Directory, wrote to the Minister:

> 'The Executive Directory, Citizen Minister, in accordance with the wish which you have so frequently expressed to resume active service with the armies, has replaced you at the Ministry of War. They entrust the portfolio of war temporarily to General Milet-Mureau. You will deliver it to him. The Directory will receive you with pleasure during your stay in Paris, in order to confer with you about the command for which they destine you.
>
> Sieyès, President'

When Bernadotte received this he wrote a letter regretting that the Directory had thought it necessary to dismiss him, but before he despatched it one of his aides-de-camp persuaded him to tear it up and write another, very different in tone. It also appeared in all the newspapers, and created quite a stir. It did not, however, result in his remaining in the ministry, though there is little reason to suppose that he was unhappy about returning to his distinguished military career.

The letter, first published in *Le Moniteur* only three days after the letter of dismissal had been written by Sieyès, is set out below:

> 'Citizen Director,
>
> 'I have received your decree and the polite letter which accompanied it. You accept a resignation which I have not given. I have on many occasions informed you about the cruel situation of my brothers in arms. Deeply afflicted at the insufficiency of the means at the disposal of the Ministry . . . I may have expressed a wish to return to the armies. . . . I have felt bound to state the facts for the sake of Truth which is beyond our control. It belongs to our contemporaries and to the verdict of history which awaits us. . . .'

Sieyès got his way but two of the members of the Directory, who were of the opinion that a very competent Minister of War had been badly treated, made an official visit to Bernadotte, in their robes, escorted by the National Guard, and told him that they were extremely annoyed at the way he had been treated by the Directory's President and thanked him for his services during his tour of duty as Minister of War.[4]

CHAPTER ELEVEN

The Brumaire coup d'état

After his retirement from the post of Minister of War Bernadotte was able to have a month's leave during which he had a complete rest which he well deserved. It was during this month that Napoleon returned from Egypt, arriving in Paris on 16 October 1799. About ten days after his arrival he met Bernadotte who had until then been trying to avoid him.

Napoleon had come back from Egypt when he did because he was afraid that during his absence Bernadotte had been climbing the ladder to power and had become even more popular with the army than he had been when Napoleon left in May 1798. Bernadotte did not want Napoleon back because he had a suspicion that all was not well with the present constitution and that another coup d'état was in the offing which might give him a great opportunity to acquire political power.

As soon as he heard the news that Napoleon had landed at Fréjus he tried to get the Directory to have him brought before a military court on charges of having deserted his army in Egypt and contravened the quarantine laws, but he received no support from Barras and nothing was done.

M. de Bourrienne, who was Napoleon's secretary, wrote in his memoirs an account of what Napoleon had said to him about Bernadotte after they had arrived at Paris.

> 'I have already learned many things; what a singular man he is! When he was Minister of War, Jourdan and others

told him that the Constitution was in danger and that it was essential that they should get rid of Sieyès, Barras and Fouché [Minister of Police] who were implicated in a conspiracy. What did he do? Nothing. He asked for proofs and no one could produce any. He asked for powers but no one would give him any. Then—he should have seized them but he did not dare.... He has Moorish blood in his veins. He is bold and enterprising. He is allied to my brothers, he does not like me and I am almost certain he will oppose me. He is so disinterested and clever.'

When he was planning the coup d'état of 18 Brumaire (8 November) Napoleon was certain, and said so, that he would have both Bernadotte and General Moreau against him. While this was going on—it was now less than a fortnight before the coup d'état took place—all the generals and politicians were doing everything they could to get on the bandwagon with the exception of Bernadotte.

It was eventually only by pressure from members of the Bonaparte family, including Joseph and his wife, Julie, who was Désirée's elder sister, that a meeting was brought about. It was rather a stormy one and when Napoleon, not tactlessly but obviously on purpose, deplored the situation in France which had worsened during his absence in Egypt, Bernadotte lost his temper. While Napoleon was not there, he told him, 'the Russians had been beaten in Switzerland and retreated to Bohemia. The line of defence between the Alps and the Appenines is maintained and we are in possession of Genoa. Holland is saved. The Russian army has been destroyed and the English army has been forced to capitulate at Helda.' He continued in this vein for some time and ended 'I do not despair of the Republic and I am convinced that she will resist her enemies both domestic and foreign.'

No one who was present during this conversation had the slightest doubt that among the 'domestic enemies' Bernadotte was including Napoleon.

In his description of the scene, Touchard-Lafosse ends by stating that at this point Madame Bonaparte tactfully changed the conversation. Another meeting was arranged by Joseph and Lucien Bonaparte but nothing embarrassing was said or done, for when the atmosphere began to get slightly overheated Josephine, as on the previous occasion, changed the subject.

By this time Bernadotte was certain that something was brewing and he had a meeting with Moreau. They gave each other certain information and exchanged views. Before they parted they agreed to join each other against Napoleon should anything happen in the near future. Chateaubriand, who later came to know Bernadotte quite well because they were both friends of Madame Récamier, and who was a great supporter of constitutional monarchy, wrote in his *Mémoires d'Outre Tombe* that when Napoleon returned from Egypt there were only four men who could prevent him from seizing power by a coup d'état; Barras, Sieyès, Moreau and Bernadotte. By this time Napoleon had taken steps to ensure that the first three would keep out of the way, but he was still warily suspicious of Bernadotte.

On 7 November, the eve of the coup d'état, Joseph left a message at Bernadotte's house in the rue Cisalpine that he would be coming to see him early the following morning. He arrived as promised and said that Napoleon wanted to see him immediately in order to ask his advice 'on the steps to be taken in the impending crisis'.[1]

When Bernadotte arrived at Napoleon's house it was full of generals including the Military Governor of Paris. As soon as Bernadotte entered the room where they all were,

Napoleon asked him why he was not in uniform, to which he replied that he was not on duty. Napoleon told him that he soon would be.

According to Lafosse, Napoleon then took Bernadotte, who had just replied that he would not soon be on duty, into the next room and told him what was about to happen. He told Bernadotte that the Directory was governing badly and would ruin the Republic unless something was done. The Council of Ancients, Napoleon said, had appointed him Commandant of Paris, the National Guards and all the troops stationed in the metropolitan area. 'Go and put your uniform on and join me as soon as possible at the Tuileries' he told Bernadotte—who refused, because he did not wish to take part in a rebellion. He tried every means in his power to get Bernadotte to change his mind but without success; and then realising that perhaps Bernadotte intended to fight on the other side he asked him to promise not to take action against him. To this Bernadotte replied, 'Yes, as a citizen I promise.' Napoleon then asked him to explain what exactly he meant by the words 'as a citizen'. He said that he would not go on his own initiative to the barracks and harangue the soldiers nor would he do anything in public to arouse or excite the National Guard or the people, but if the Directory were to call on him to take command of the Guard *he would be prepared* [author's italics] to take the field against those who were seeking to overthrow the lawful constitution.

The following day, 19 Brumaire, was to be D-day. Great risks were being run although some of the conspirators did not seem to realise it. Sieyès, however, was not completely confident that all would go well and his horses were harnessed all day to his carriage which remained near the Palais de St Cloud so that he could get away should the coup d'état fail. Bourriene, according to the historian Vandal, when driving through the Place de la Concorde with one of Napoleon's aides de camp, pointed to where the guillotine so often used to be set up during the Reign of Terror and said, 'Tomorrow we shall either sleep at the Luxembourg Palace or we shall finish up here.'

Napoleon, however, appeared to be in fine fettle and quite confident. Those who were opposed to the coup, and they included a large majority of the Council of Five Hundred, had no leader. They had, however, complete confidence in Bernadotte who was extremely popular with the troops, all the more so because of the way in which he had been dismissed from his appointment of Minister of War. Furthermore, there were very few generals who could more profoundly influence the troops by making a speech to them. There are plenty of examples already in this book that he was a master of that.

On this occasion, however, he was being very cautious and was not prepared to take any action against the leaders and supporters of the coup d'état without an order from the Legislature or some other high authority.

Nevertheless he is supposed to have made this offer to the Council.[2]

> 'Let one of you ascend the tribune and describe succinctly the external and internal situation of France. He will be able to prove easily that we are in a position to obtain a peace as honourable as that of Campo Formio, and in order to maintain such a peace we have only to preserve the commanding position which we occupy. After having pointed out that Bonaparte's investiture by a fraction of the Council of Ancients is a violation of the Constitution, disclaim on the part of the Council of the Five Hundred any intention of discussing the violation, but only of giving

> security to the nation, the Legislature and the Government. Propose, with this object in view, that the Council of Five Hundred shall appoint General Bernadotte to be the colleague of General Bonaparte so that the two generals can act in concert in employing armed force, if it becomes necessary to have recourse to such force, and in the distribution of commands. Conclude by giving an assurance that tranquillity reigns in Paris and its vicinity, which justifies the presumption that there will be no necessity to bring the troops into action.'

'Send me such a decree,' said Bernadotte, 'and twenty minutes after its receipt I shall be with my aides-de-camp in your midst. I shall take command of the corps I shall meet in my path and we shall then see what there is to be done. If it is necessary to proclaim Bonaparte an outlaw you will have at your side a general and, at the very least, a great portion of the troops.'

The Council did not give him any authority and he spent the day far away from the centre of Paris wondering what was happening and what was the result of the coup. Meanwhile a lot was happening at the Palais de St Cloud and Napoleon was having quite a difficult time. The Directory consisted of the Council of Ancients and the Council of Five Hundred; the former were due to meet in the gallery of Apollo and the latter in the Orangerie at noon, but owing to some delay they were about an hour late.

The question has often been asked whether there was anything Bernadotte could have done had he been there. The answer mostly depends on what troops were at the time stationed in or around the palaces, because without their support he could have done nothing. There were some troops, who formed the guard of the Directory and of the Council, who would certainly have followed him but there were others, some dragoons and infantry of the line, upon whom Napoleon could have counted.

When in session on 19 Brumaire a majority of the Ancients were on Napoleon's side but they were not sufficiently enthusiastic to take any definite action. The Council of Five Hundred, however, were strongly against any coup d'état. Napoleon addressed both chambers without any success whatsoever and in the Council of Five Hundred he was assaulted by some of the members and threatened with outlawry.

The judgement of most French historians regarding the attitude of Bernadotte to the coup of 18–19 Brumaire is that it was entirely due to animosity and jealousy towards Napoleon. Vandal's opinion is that it was a fault in his character, namely that he was too hesitant to join in the coup and too ambitious to be dragged into it. On the other hand Napoleon had 'faith in his star'.

Bernadotte was much less proud of himself and was able to see the possible dangers of the coup's failure. Were it to succeed he did not think that there would be much difficulty in jumping on the band-wagon, whereas if it did not come off he would be in a wonderful position. There is reason to believe, however, that his attitude was not entirely based on reason. His heart had something to do with it. Had it not been for the fact that his wife Désirée was very fond of her sister Julie, Joseph Bonaparte's wife, it is more than likely that he would have opposed the coup in which event it might easily have gone the other way. Bourienne, in his memoirs, stated that 'family considerations' probably had some effect on Bernadotte's decision to remain aloof.

When at last Bernadotte received information that the coup had been a success there was nothing for him and his wife to do but leave Paris and go into hiding as quickly as possible, for the police were known to be searching for all Napoleon's opponents. First and foremost of these were the Jacobins including one of their most important leaders, General Jourdan. Many of them were condemned to be deported.

General Sarrazin, who had served under Bernadotte on many occasions, gave an account of what he found on the night of the coup when he arrived home. He was astonished to see Bernadotte and a little youth whom he did not at first recognise but who turned out to be Désirée dressed in boy's clothes. Bernadotte told him that after giving much thought to the question of where would be the best place to hide until Napoleon cooled off from his first fit of rage, he decided to come to his old friend, both because he felt certain that Sarrazin would keep his secret and because the Chateau Fraguier, Sarrazin's house, was close to the forest of Senart where it would be easy for his wife and himself to hide with the certainty of not wanting the means of living. 'I thanked him,' wrote Sarrazin, 'for having given me the preference, and assured him that his confidence would be amply justified.'

They only stayed there for three days during which time Joseph did his best to get his brother to forgive Bernadotte so that he could return to the bosom of the family.

CHAPTER TWELVE

Interlude in Paris

As a result of the coup all the executive powers of the Directory were handed over to a new organisation called the Provisional Consulate of which Napoleon was a member; on 12 November they took an oath to be 'faithful to the Republic'. Napoleon's brother Joseph had meanwhile been successful in securing his promise that Bernadotte would be in no danger if he returned to Paris. Later the new government formally gave him a pardon, and also his followers.

It was on Christmas Day 1799 that the final result of the coup took place. The Provisional Consulate ceased to exist and a new Executive was set up under a First Consul who would hold office for ten years. Napoleon became First Consul and had the sole power to appoint all ministers, ambassadors and other principal officers of state.

The new government consisted of three Houses of Parliament—the Senate, the Legislative Body and the Tribunate. Napoleon, who as First Consul was determined to be head of everything, then set up a fourth organisation which he called the Conseil d'Etat, composed of the Consuls, the ministers and about forty members who were not elected but nominated. This Conseil d'Etat therefore gave Napoleon virtually complete control of the whole state; he was in effect dictator, which is what he wanted. While all this was going on Bernadotte kept quiet and expressed no criticism at all of what Napoleon was doing. He was very wise, because he knew that he had the Bonaparte family behind him and it would have been foolish to have done anything which would have lost him their support.

By the middle of January 1800 he was offered and accepted a seat in the Conseil d'Etat. Being by nature first and foremost a soldier it was not long before he became extremely bored with what was nothing more than a political appointment and he was longing to get back to the army. France was at war with Austria and Napoleon could not, because he was First Consul, command any army stationed in the Republic. He therefore offered the command of his army to Bernadotte. Before he actually took over, however, something more attractive arose. The English Channel was reported to be full of British men-of-war and it was assumed that there would shortly be an attempted invasion of France by a British army. Bernadotte thought that this was just the job for him and suggested to the First Consul that he should be appointed C-in-C of what was called the Western Command. The appointment only lasted for a couple of months, and since no real invasion took place all Bernadotte had to do was to round up a number of royalist rebels in the Vendée, about the only region of France where the royalist leaders still had considerable influence. It was not what Bernadotte expected he would have to do and he did not enjoy it.

There was some trouble in Tours, where in September there had been a mutiny in the 52nd Regiment, and Bernadotte gave orders to the local commander that the ringleaders were to be arrested and brought before a military tribunal. A despatch was sent to the Minister of War reporting the orders which had been given.

He had without doubt taken the right action but Napoleon thought that it was a good opportunity to criticise Bernadotte; he ordered his secretary Bourienne to make the following note in the margin of the despatch which had been sent to the Minister of War: 'General Bernadotte has acted wrongly in taking such measures against the 52nd Regiment, not having the requisite means of enforcing the order in the centre of a town where the garrison is insufficient to keep the mob in check.' It is not difficult to imagine what the First Consul's comment would have been had Bernadotte taken no action at all.

Shortly after this incident Bernadotte was given leave and went to Paris. He was extremely bored with the Western Command and somehow or other he persuaded Napoleon to appoint him C-in-C of a new army which was just being formed to proceed to Italy to reinforce the troops already there. Having made this appointment he then offered Murat the Western Command in succession to Bernadotte which enraged Murat so much that he wrote the following letter to Joseph Bonaparte.

> 'My dear Joseph—Lucien has left for Madrid. A thousand absurd rumours are current about the motive of his departure. Louis is also absent and now they wish to get rid of me. The First Consul has proposed—would you believe it possible—to appoint me to the command of the Army of the West and he has done so because he wished to give the Army of the Reserve, which had been destined for me, to Bernadotte. I have refused point-blank and on the day on which Bernadotte is preferred to me I shall hand in my resignation. I shall never endure tranquilly the spectacle of power passing into the hands of the man who, on the 18 Brumaire, was on the side of those who voted outlawry against our family.
>
> Joachim Murat'

Murat could speak of 'our family', for Caroline Bonaparte was his wife. His letter caused Napoleon to change his mind and he cancelled Bernadotte's appointment and gave it to Murat.

In a letter which Bernadotte then wrote to Joseph he asked him to speak to his brother and remind him how much he wanted to be given an active command because he was a soldier, not a politician. He said how much he wanted to get away from Paris and explained why. 'The political parties begin to agitate, clubs are being formed, the Royalists are numerous and an opposition to them is being organised. Paris is a sewer in which all the impurities and corruption find a refuge. Help me, dear Joseph, to escape from Paris in some honourable way.'[1]

Bernadotte managed to get away from Paris and in 'an honourable way'; but it was not the one he wanted. All that happened was that he went back to his command in Brittany and La Vendée. On his return he thought it would be a good idea to try to get his troops to regard the inhabitants of those regions as fellow countrymen. It would make it less likely that troubles and fights between the army and the locals would take place. He therefore issued the following Order of the Day.

> 'Soldiers of the Army of the West, you have fought with me in Germany, where you invariably respected the Germans and their property. In Italy your enemies were forced to admire the order and discipline which you always observed. In France you must not carry desolation into the bosom of those families whose children were covered with glory on the plains of Marengo under the First Consul Bonaparte. Do not believe those pretended patriots who seek to embitter you against those brother soldiers who

thought themselves obliged by honour and duty to fight in defence of the throne and the altar. Peace happily is restored, every illusion is dissipated; there are no longer Chouans or Vendeans. We are all Frenchmen.'

Before the end of February an opportunity arose which gave Bernadotte the hope that before long he might be posted to a more interesting command. This was the signing of the Treaty of Lunéville between France and Austria. This meant that the only countries in Europe which were likely to be at war in the near future were France and England, and it was therefore more likely that Napoleon would before long be able to declare war on England and to invade the British Isles since France would no longer have to fight a war on two fronts.

To be appointed C-in-C of the French invasion army was just what Bernadotte wanted as he made quite clear in a letter to Lucien Bonaparte a fortnight after the Treaty of Lunéville had been signed.

'My dear Lucien, I have wished for a long time to write to you. . . . I await the dissolution of the active armies when I shall know for certain whether I am to take the field in command of an army destined for the campaign against England. If this hope is disappointed I shall leave France for our dominions across the seas in order to seek the happiness which is denied to me in my own country by men who owe me justice and recognition.'

The expectation of an invasion in the near future was confirmed by a report sent from Paris to the British Foreign Office, dated 10 July 1801.[2] In short, it stated that two expeditions against England were being planned and that Bernadotte and Massena would be in command of them. It also mentioned the names of two other generals, Augereau and

Brune, who would also most probably have commands. The reasons for Napoleon having selected these men were that they were able and experienced generals, and that he disliked them for personal reasons and was perfectly prepared to sacrifice them.

The main landing was expected somewhere on the coast of Essex with two feints on the coasts of Kent and Sussex. It was also intended, the report stated, that combined French and Spanish fleets should put to sea about the same time with a large body of troops aboard. The report also gave the names of the two admirals who would be in command of the fleets and stated that at the moment of the report's being written they were both in Paris 'concerting with the Government the Plan of Operations'.

No invasion, of course, took place and on 1 October, as the result of negotiations between England and France, 'Preliminaries of Peace' were signed. These were soon followed by the Peace of Amiens in March 1802, after which the Army of the West was disbanded.

No longer able to rely on Russia, Napoleon felt bound temporarily to give up his great plan. Each of the signatories, however, had mental reservations. England, who promised to evacuate Malta, had no intention of doing so while Napoleon did not give up his dream of a continental blockade. Many English historians have accused Addington, who had only just become Prime Minister before the treaty was signed, of having surrendered too much, but most French writers think differently. At any rate England retained what was, perhaps, more important than anything else, her naval supremacy.[3] Three and a half years later this was responsible for the great victory of Trafalgar. Nevertheless from Bernadotte's point of view the disbandment of the Army of the West was a great disappointment. He was not given another command, nor was he impressed by being given permission by Napoleon to retain the title and pay of a GOC while he remained unemployed.

While Bernadotte was in Paris before the 18 Brumaire coup d'état until about the middle of 1802 he became quite a notable person in Parisian society and was liked and admired by three of the best-known hostesses, Madame de Staël, Madame Récamier, and Madame de Genlis. Madame de Genlis wrote of him that he looked astonishingly like the portraits of the great Condé. 'His fine appearance, the nobleness of his manners and his politeness aided the resemblance which he completed in other respects.'

He was not what one would call good-looking since his long Béarnais nose was too prominent to make him attractive, but he possessed great charm and his looks could properly be described as striking. Apart from his presence and his conversational fascination, he had a great reputation as a brave and successful general.

Madame de Staël first met Bernadotte in 1797 when she was already being watched by spies because she was regarded as a counter-revolutionary. She had been banned from the capital but on 19 Brumaire, the second day of the coup d'état, she returned to Paris although without the permission of the government. Shortly after her return Napoleon managed to win her over by appointing her great friend Benjamin Constant a member of the Tribunate, but it was not long before Napoleon became dissatisfied with this assembly and he had Constant deprived of his membership. This infuriated the 'Mistress to an age', as Madame de Staël is sometimes called, and she at once became a member of the opposition which was generally known as the anti-Napoleonists. From then on she saw a great deal of Bernadotte because, in so far as Napoleon was concerned, they had much in common.

Napoleon was extremely annoyed and not a little suspicious of their friendship and early in 1802 she was exiled. The actual cause was the Concordat which Napoleon had signed with Pope Pius VII and which was due to come into effect when the Catholic clergy were restored and the First Consul was nominated for life. Republicans and royalists felt that they had been betrayed by the man on whom they pinned their hopes and it was at this stage that Madame de Staël made her drawing room a meeting place for the leaders of both these parties.

When Napoleon was in exile on St Helena, he was reported to have said, while reminiscing about Madame de Staël, that 'at the time of the Concordat she suddenly united the aristocrats and royalists against me, "You have not a moment to waste", she said to them, "tomorrow the tyrant will have 40,000 priests at his command."'

She also knew all about the Conspiracy of Paris (January–April 1802) and even if she were not one of the conspirators, she was at least an aider and abettor. As she herself has written, 'After the purging of the Tribunate there formed around Bernadotte a party of Generals and Senators who encouraged him to form resolutions against the usurpation which was advancing at rapid strides.' The conspiracy never became a danger to the First Consul because it never took any action.

Bernadotte's real friendship with Madame Récamier began early in 1801. She stated many years later that her relations with Bernadotte dated from an event too serious and too sad ever to be forgotten. 'The services which he rendered to me at that time can never be effaced from the tablets of my memory,' she wrote. This was a reference to a party which she gave one night in February 1801 at her house in Paris in honour of Napoleon's eldest sister, during which news arrived that Madame Récamier's father had been arrested on a charge of distributing Royalist propaganda. Shortly afterwards her guest of honour left and went with her sister to the Théâtre Français. Madame Récamier shortly followed her there to ask whether, as Napoleon's sister, she could help her in any way, which she promised to do as soon as the play was over.

They were in a box and as Madame Récamier was too upset to watch the play she went into a dark corner of it and sat down to wait. She told the rest of the story in her memoirs.[5]

> 'Suddenly I noticed that in the opposite corner of the box there was a man whose dark eyes were fixed on me with an expression of such deep interest and compassion that I was greatly moved. After having experienced so much coldness, it was a relief to meet with a little sympathy and kindness. At that moment another sister of Napoleon, Madame Pauline Leclerc, turned to me and asked if I had ever previously seen the actor Lafon play the part of Achilles and without even waiting for an answer she added "He is very handsome but today he is wearing a most unbecoming tunic." At this idle question, showing so much indifference to my state of feelings (for she was perfectly aware that my father had been arrested and taken to the Temple [prison]) the unknown man made an involuntary movement of impatience, and, doubtless having made up his mind to shorten my punishment, he leant forwards toward Madame Bacciochi [Napoleon's sister, for whom the party had been given] and said in a low voice: "Madame Récamier seems to be in pain. If she will allow me I shall take her home and promise to speak to the First Consul." "Certainly," said Madame Bacciochi, delighted to escape the task, "Nothing could be more fortunate for you,

Madame. Put your trust in General Bernadotte. Nobody is in a better position to serve you." I hastened to accept General Bernadotte's offer.

'I took his left arm and left the theatre with him. He took me to my carriage and sat beside me ordering his carriage to follow. During the journey he did his best to reassure me as to my father's fate and so often repeated that he hoped to get Napoleon to stop the prosecution that I arrived home somewhat consoled. He then left for the Tuileries, promising to bring me word the same evening, whatsoever answer he might receive.... I counted the minutes until he returned. He came at last happy and triumphant. By means of his pressure he had obtained from the First Consul the promise that my father would not be put on trial, and he hoped that he would soon be set at liberty. I lacked words sufficient to thank him.... Bernadotte did not abandon the task he had undertaken. One morning he came holding in his hand the order for my father's release which he presented to me with that chivalrous grace which characterised him. He asked me, as his only recompense, the favour of accompanying me to the Temple to see the prisoner discharged.'

After the Peace of Amiens there was, not surprisingly, a large number of generals without any command, and many staff officers and several thousand junior officers, all of whom naturally put the blame on Napoleon whom, for the first time, they called 'Le Petit Caporal'. They thought, and they were quite right to do so, that Napoleon had fought as they had done for the new Republic so long as it suited him, but now they had begun to realise that republicanism meant nothing to him and that his goal was to become the head of state. The two leaders of these disgruntled officers were Generals

Moreau and Bernadotte but they were very careful to do nothing that could be construed as a breach of the constitution. Other officers, however, including two cavalry colonels named Donnadieu and Fournier, were not so prudent which led to their arrest on a charge of 'conspiring to assassinate the First Consul'. It became known as the Donnadieu Conspiracy. Napoleon did all he could to implicate Moreau and Bernadotte but there was not a shred of evidence to justify their arrest and Donnadieu and Fournier were never brought to trial.

Within a couple of weeks, however, another conspiracy had taken place which became known as the 'Plot of the Placards'. Once again there was absolutely no evidence to implicate Bernadotte although Napoleon suspected that he was involved and actually told some of his friends that he intended to have him shot. He did not really think that his enemy number one was involved in the plot but tried hard to find a job for him which would ensure his being well out of the way for the time being. He offered him the post of Governor of Louisiana, the earliest settlers of which were Frenchmen and which derived its name from Louis XIV. Louis XV had handed it over to Spain for a sum of money but it had recently been returned to France.

When the appointment became known to the British Foreign Office a report was sent to it by a Mr Merry stating that 'when Bernadotte proceeds to Louisiana (which will be as soon as the armaments can be prepared) he is to take possession, at the same time, of the Floridas.'[6] Bernadotte was pleased with the idea of being sent to Louisiana for two reasons, firstly because he thought it would be a very interesting job and might eventually lead to better things and secondly because he would be miles away and in a different continent from the First Consul.

But he made it a condition of his accepting the post that 3,000 soldiers and an equal number of agriculturists should be placed at his disposal and maintained by France for two years after which time he would assume responsibility for them himself. As Napoleon refused to accept these conditions Bernadotte turned down the offer. Almost immediately after this Napoleon, obviously still wishing to get Bernadotte out of the way, offered him the appointment of Ambassador Plenipotentiary to the United States of America which he accepted, but he delayed his departure until Napoleon gave him orders to leave for Washington immediately.

Bernadotte, however, did not know at that time that Napoleon had decided to sell Louisiana to the United States for eighty million francs (which was then about £3,200,000). Such a sum of money would be most useful to enable him to meet the expenses of the war which was just about to begin. Just when Bernadotte with Désirée were about to sail to the United States from La Rochelle, he read in *Le Moniteur* that the negotiations for the sale had just come to a conclusion, that Lord Whitworth the English Ambassador had left on 12 May and that on 16 May war had been declared between France and England.

Bernadotte at once wrote to Joseph Bonaparte enclosing with his letter one for the First Consul.

'On my arrival at La Rochelle I read in *Le Moniteur* the declaration of war by England. Fate seems to have pursued me for a long time and to be always placing me without any fault of my own in opposition to the intentions of the First Consul. The course of events compels me to ask him to allow me to return to my military duties. Before he became a civil magistrate he was a General and no one will be better able than he to judge that duty, honour and delicacy of feeling have prompted me to make this request of him. If, in spite of my efforts, my enemies endeavour to set him against me, I appeal to you, my dear Joseph, to point out to him that no blame can justly attach to me, since two frigates which were detailed to take me to the States were employed for other purposes and the third for which I am waiting here in La Rochelle cannot sail for a fortnight.... I hope to be restored to the position of which I have been deprived by the influence of those who are the jealous enemies of your fortunes and of mine. You will be able to bring all my claims before the General and to ask him to give me a command. You know what I wish for most of all. If your occupation proves unsuccessful I shall retire to the country and live as a peaceful citizen. I embrace you and beg you to forward the enclosed letter to the Consul.

J. B. Bernadotte'

The enclosed letter was as follows:

> 'General, on my arrival at La Rochelle I have been informed of public events which lead me to regard my mission at an end; and I see in *Le Moniteur* that England has declared war against France. I offer to the Government my services and my sword. I leave for Paris tomorrow.'

Both the above letters were written on 27 May 1803.

Napoleon, like Queen Victoria on a notable occasion, was not amused, but he was sensible enough to realise that now that his country was at war with England Bernadotte would never leave it except as a soldier.

CHAPTER THIRTEEN

The Empire

The war between France and England which had been predicted did not lead to immediate action, and all that Napoleon did was to occupy the Kingdom of Hanover in May 1804. Bernadotte hoped, though perhaps he did not really expect, to get some kind of command, but he was to be disappointed as General Mortier was appointed Commander-in-Chief.

For more than a year Bernadotte continued to be unemployed and lived in his country house at La Grange. A few months before this, however, there had been a royalist conspiracy in which General Moreau was involved and brought to trial with other leading conspirators. Most of them were sentenced to death but Moreau, much to Napoleon's disgust, was only sentenced to two years imprisonment.

Napoleon had during the past few months received information from his police and agents-provocateurs that there was a likelihood that there would soon be a royalist revolt in Normandy and Brittany and that on the arrival of a certain Bourbon prince the explosion would take place. Accordingly the Duc d'Enghien, the last descendant of the House of Condé, was kidnapped on 21 March 1804, taken to Vincennes and then secretly shot on Napoleon's orders.

This crime, appalling because the Duc d'Enghien had not been involved in the conspiracy, produced the effect which the First Consul intended it to have. The Bourbon princes never took any further steps to get rid of Napoleon and the republicans no longer suspected, as some of them had done, that he was pro-royalist. He had joined the regicides; the only thing he really thought of was supreme power for himself. About this time, owing to some information which Désirée had given Napoleon, he sent for Bernadotte in order that he could discuss the possible future.

Madame Récamier stated in her memoirs that on this occasion when he was summoned to the Tuileries Bernadotte was rather worried as he suspected that Napoleon wanted to see him because he was determined to implicate Bernadotte in the royalist conspiracy. After the interview was over he gave an account of it to Madame Récamier. He told her that the interview was not about what he had expected but that Napoleon had proposed an alliance between them.

'You see,' Napoleon said, referring to the royalist conspiracy, 'that the question has been decided in my favour. The nation has chosen me, not the Bourbons, but she needs the co-operation of all her children. Will you march forward with me and with all our country?' Bernadotte told Madame Récamier that he had obviously no alternative but to say yes. 'I promised him loyal co-operation and told him that I would keep my word.'

About ten days later Napoleon created fourteen marshals, most of whom he was sure he could rely on, although five of them were true republicans who had at one time been opposed to him. Among the five were Massena, Jourdan and Bernadotte whom Napoleon thought it was most important to have on his side.

It was on 18 May that a Senatus Consultum conferred on Napoleon the title of Emperor of the French. On the day of the proclamation the new marshals were the first to be received by the new Emperor. Although he had given his solemn promise to recognise Napoleon as Emperor and support him, it was a great shock to Bernadotte, however much he preferred the new Empire to a restoration of the Bourbons. He felt that he wanted to tell somebody of his disappointment and he chose Lucien Bonaparte who had not been on friendly terms with his brother Napoleon for the last seven months.

> 'I take an opportunity, my dear Senator, to have a frank talk with you, without exposing myself to the risks of the Post Office, which friend Fouché increases every day.* If it had not been for that consideration I should have written sooner, but I prefer that my letters should reach their destination and I know that they forward nothing which displeases them. What do you say about the event of the moment? What do you think of this so-called "Senatus Consultum"? A pretty business that. Your monk Sieyès, who deluded you and Joseph with his famous constitution [this was a reference to the Directory] did not foresee this crown of his edifice. He must, however, have apprehended something of the kind, since he conceived the idea of what he called "absorption", a sort of metaphysical notion which he designed in order to prevent a popular leader from aspiring to or seizing power. But General Bonaparte with good reasons willed otherwise. In truth, instead of Bonaparte being absorbed it is we poor soldiers, who have done nothing for our country, as everyone knows, except shed our blood for her, who have been literally "absorbed". As a result there will be no more glory except near him, with him, by him, and unfortunately for him. Since it has pleased the sovereign people to despoil them-

* On Fouché's orders letters were frequently opened. This letter was taken by hand by a friend of Bernadotte who was returning to Italy.

selves in favour of an Emperor it has doubtless been on an implied condition, that he will give them peace. . . . and you will see how they will get it. It will be a case of "Forward soldiers. Long live the Emperor", instead of "Long live the Republic". That will be a far more effective battle-cry. You know, Lucien, that I am your friend, and that I did my best to dissuade you from surrendering your position and from abandoning public life. I told you on the night before your departure that the man who gives up the game loses it, and that instead of silently effacing yourself you had only to say the word, in order to revive what would deserve the name of a party. Your friends and mine say that you were guilty of weakness or of complicity with your brother. But I know that on 19 Brumaire you only acted a fraternal part when you ought to have had the courage to put to the vote in your capacity of President of the Council of Five Hundred, the outlawry of that brother who violated by force of arms the national representation. Yes, you betrayed your duty and your republican conscience—because nobody knows better than you that the decree of outlawry was deserved. Have you no genuine admiration for those great men of antiquity, the two Brutuses and Timoleon? They were cases of father and son and brother and brother, and that is why their names will remain for ever celebrated. The General would not have been guilty of any such pusillanimity in your favour if your situations had been reversed. But have I any right to reproach you for not having imitated the grand models of which history gives us examples, since I was found wanting also—thanks to the persuasion of Joseph? Why? Because Joseph is the husband of Julie who is the sister of my wife Désirée. On such trifles depend the destinies of a great Empire. You know that the Faubourg of

St Antoine was on my side. We had armies and we had men—who under my orders would not have been his tools. But no. Everything went wrong on that day. Weakness alone triumphed thanks to you in the beginning, and thanks to me for allowing myself to be captured by fine words, when perhaps I might have prevented it all. Nevertheless I had begun to reconcile myself to the Consular Republic although it was but a mutilated variety of the constitution of your Abbé. Today it is gone. Now we are imperialised by a plebiscite. I wonder what the Canon of Chrone [Sieyès] thinks of it. They say he has grown fat, while he laughs at you and me and all the world, except the Emperor Napoleon and himself. If, in the Senate or outside it, one of the old veterans of 1789 had dared to say to a nation which was intoxicated by the prestige of a glory to which we had helped to accustom them: "Pause my friends. Do you wish to experience once more that royalty which you drenched in the blood of the unfortunate Louis XVI? (your hypocritical Abbé can tell you all about that[1])—well, deliver yourselves over hand and foot to an absolute despotism. Look at your neighbours the English. After killing one king, they took another. But he was a constitutional king who if he could not do much good, could at least not do much harm."

'Absolute monarchy is a master which in its own interest requires to be disarmed. Nothing is more dangerous than absolute power which produces these paroxysms that are called revolutions of which kings are generally the first victims.... They wish to see you far away from France. Rome is too near. ... They would like to see you in the place where they have sent Moreau, whither, perhaps, they would perhaps like to send me. I am holding my ground. I wish to obtain a certain command through Joseph who retains some influence over Caesar. Perhaps when I am at a distance I shall no longer provoke hatred. In any case I am unwilling to repose under the shade of another's laurels. If I cannot do better I shall retire to America—perhaps to be followed by you.

'Farewell. Take care of your health in that fever-laden climate. Present my homage to Madame Lucien, and do not allow her to give way to the despondency which General Lacour tells me has afflicted her. She is too beautiful and too good to excite the hatred of anyone; and she is too wise not to understand that she is only the pretext of your banishment. Napoleon would thank her, if he dared, for having furnished him with it. Goodbye, Lucien—Au revoir—when and where God pleases.

J. B. Bernadotte'[2]

CHAPTER FOURTEEN

Hanover

Shortly after he became Emperor and had received Bernadotte's promise of loyalty, Napoleon appointed Bernadotte to be Governor and Commander-in-Chief of the Electorate of Hanover which still belonged to the English crown although it had been occupied by the French since 1803, after the breakdown of the Treaty of Amiens.

While on the way to Hanover to take over the governorship Bernadotte paid a visit to the two large camps at Boulogne and Ostend which were under the command of Marshal Davout, another general with whom he was not on the best of terms, to put it mildly. The main reason for this was that at the time of the Donnadieu conspiracy Davout had been chief of Napoleon's Military Police and had supplied the First Consul with certain information in the hope that it might implicate Bernadotte.

At this time Sir George Rumbold was the British Ambassador in Hamburg and in June and July 1804 he had sent a series of reports to the British Foreign Office about Bernadotte's arrival in the Electorate. As a result of this and other evidence of what the French considered espionage the Minister of Police, Fouché, sent a letter to Bernadotte on 1 October.

> 'I have strong evidence, Marshal, that an English Agent at Hamburg, Rumbold, has been following the same prac-

tice of espionage and intrigue which have excited the indignation of Europe against the Drakes and the Spencer Smiths [Spencer Smith was a diplomat]. It is clear that the British Government has dared to avow and even to systematise these tactics of conspiracy on the part of their Ministers who are accredited to allied or neutral powers. In this way their Ministers are, so to speak, made conspirators, and are placed outside the common law of civilised nations. It is the express order of the Emperor that Mr. (sic) Rumbold be seized and that possession be taken of all papers found in his house. I therefore write to you, Marshal, to take all steps necessary for carrying out that operation as promptly as possible.

Fouché'

On 24 October Sir George was arrested and taken to Paris and kept in the famous Temple Prison in Paris for several months before being released at the request of the King of Prussia.

On 24 December 1804 Napoleon was crowned at Nôtre Dame in Paris and Bernadotte, who took part in the procession, carried the collar of the Emperor. For the time being, at any rate, the Emperor's attitude towards Bernadotte appeared to be getting more friendly; less than a month after the coronation he was given a residence in the rue d'Anjou in Paris.

During his period as Governor and Commander-in-Chief of the occupation troops in Hanover, Bernadotte became most popular and this undoubtedly had something to do with his eventually becoming King of Sweden. A member of the government of Hanover wrote that 'his nobility of character, his generosity and his humanity were so universally recognised that the inhabitants preferred a French occupation under him to a Prussian occupation which they had good reason to apprehend'.[1]

Many other examples of his generosity and humanity have been given by various writers. One of them refers to an incident which took place during a military review; a lady in Hanover was watching the review when 'the horses of her carriage shied and endangered the safety of the occupants. Marshal Bernadotte, who happened to be standing near, mounted his horse and galloped away to stop the firing.'[2] Bernadotte was even successful in persuading the Emperor to permit him to be more lenient to the Hanoverians than some other governors were allowed to be. Eventually he obtained a reduction in the size of the army of occupation by three regiments, which not only saved a lot of money on its upkeep but also released 200 tons of wheat. He had to take steps to ensure that none of it would be sent to England with which the Hanoverians, during the occupation, were not allowed to trade.

CHAPTER FIFTEEN

The Grand Army

While Bernadotte was in Hanover Napoleon was setting up the invasion camp at Boulogne which most people, and particularly the British government, thought was intended as a base for the invasion of England. At the end of August 1805, however, he decided to attack Austria in order to defeat the Austrian forces before they could join up with the Russians who were already marching towards Ulm in order to help them.

It was for the attack on Austria that the famous Grand Army was formed and given that name on 25 August. It consisted of about 200,000 men divided into seven Army Corps, Bernadotte's corps being stationed in Hanover and forming the left wing of the Army. In order that the new invasion of Austria should come as a surprise there was a cover-plan which was conveyed to Bernadotte by Napoleon's Chief of Staff, Marshal Berthier, in the following order:

> 'Your movements in the present state of public opinion will attract curiosity. You must, therefore, be careful to announce that it is your intention to winter in Hanover. In fact, after reviewing your troops at Göttingen you will return immediately to your capital. The Emperor cannot leave you in ignorance of the fact that negotiations are pending with Prussia and that it is necessary to put that Court on the wrong scent so that they may not realise the Emperor's plan of collecting all his forces.'

Berthier sent another order shortly afterwards instructing Bernadotte to announce that he was returning to France and that other troops would relieve the Army of Hanover.

The cover-plan was not successful because in a document sent to the British Foreign Office by a British agent in Berlin it was reported on 10 September that Bernadotte's Army Corps 'is destined to join that of Marmont and to act against Austria'.[1] This report was, of course, absolutely true. In a letter which Napoleon wrote to Bernadotte on 27 September he predicted that before 12 October Austria could be defeated.

> 'From Wurtzburg you will make for the Danube in accordance with instructions which the Minister of War will send you this evening. I have made an offensive and defensive alliance with the Elector of Bavaria. His army is at my disposal. . . . You are by this time at Wurtsburg and the Elector's fears must be at an end. You know the esteem and friendship I bear you. Now is the moment to strike a decisive blow. Before the 12 October Austria will be defeated.—Napoleon'[2]

At the battle of Austerlitz on 2 December, which Napoleon regarded as his greatest victory, an army of more than 80,000 Russians and Austrians was overwhelmingly defeated, suffering according to official estimates, 30,000 casualties and a loss of 186 guns. It also terminated the alliance between Russia and Austria.

CHAPTER SIXTEEN

Anspach, Jena and Lübeck

After the Battle of Austerlitz Bernadotte was appointed Governor of Anspach while Berthier remained in Germany as Commander-in-Chief of the Grand Army; as usual Bernadotte during his governorship was both popular and successful.

Napoleon during the next six months spent most of his time giving his relations, friends and some of his generals, thrones, princedoms and dukedoms. His brother Joseph became the King of Naples, his Chief of Staff Berthier was given the Princedom of Neuchatel and his brother-in-law Murat was made Grand Duke of Cleves, to mention only some of them.

He had also decided to give something to Bernadotte and while he was considering what to give him an opportunity arose from a disagreement between King Joseph and the Vatican in respect of two small states on the frontier of the Kingdom of Naples, Benevento and Ponte Corvo. On 6 July, therefore, under Letters Patent he conferred on Bernadotte the title of Prince and Duke of Ponte Corvo 'to possess it in full proprietorship and sovereignty and as an immediate fief of our Crown'.

In the Letters Patent it was clearly stated that the reason for conferring this title on 'his cousin Marshal Bernadotte' was because Napoleon wanted to give the Marshal a testimony of his gratitude for his cousin's services rendered to the Crown. In a letter which Napoleon wrote to his brother Joseph,[1] however, he made it clear that he had bestowed the title of Prince of Ponte Corvo upon Bernadotte 'out of consideration for your wife . . . I have felt that it would be suitable for the brother-in-law of the Queen of Naples to have a distinguished rank at your court'.

Incidentally, Ponte Corvo was a very small principality with only sixty thousand inhabitants, but it made Bernadotte a prince. When later he became the Crown Prince of Sweden it was not, perhaps, such a jump as it would have seemed had he still been only a Marshal of France.

Very soon after he was made Prince of Ponte Corvo, an incident took place on the eve of the Battle of Jena which was highly embarrassing for Bernadotte. When all the facts are considered objectively, it was perhaps no more than a serious error of judgement, though a most unfortunate one, for it resulted in his being absent from this crucial battle. The real reason for his not arriving there on time was the justified misunderstanding of an order issued by Napoleon's Chief of Staff. Nevertheless, despite this misunderstanding he could have reached the battlefield on time if the battle had not been fought a day earlier than was expected even by Napoleon himself.

Immediately after the battle,[2] however, Bernadotte had an opportunity to make up for his unfortunate mistake when, in company with Marshals Murat and Soult, he took a very active part in the pursuit of the defeated Prussian army and particularly during the attack on Halle.

The capture of Halle was one of Bernadotte's greatest achievements—which is saying a great deal, for there were many of them. The town was a walled fortress on the northern bank of the river Saale, backed by a range of hills, and was defended by about 20,000 Prussian troops. Many generals would not have attempted to attack the town and would have preferred to besiege it until eventually the garrison surrendered. Not Bernadotte, however, who was determined to attack the town on 17 October. Before night set in the Prussians retreated leaving behind more than 6,000 killed, 6,000 prisoners and 30 guns.[3]

A few days later Napoleon reached Halle and had a good look at the town and its fortifications. He is reported as saying that he did not think he would have attacked the town with less than 50,000 troops, but, he added, 'Bernadotte hesitates at nothing. One of these days the Gascon will be caught.'[4] By 23 October the Prussians were really on the run northwards pursued by the armies of three Marshals—Soult on the left flank, Murat on the right and Bernadotte in the centre. Thirteen days later, on 5 November, they reached Lübeck where there were 25,000 troops under Blücher (who nine years later with the Duke of Wellington administered the final defeat to Napoleon at Waterloo). Once Blücher's force in Lübeck was surrounded by the French there was no possibility of their escaping.

Bernadotte made the main attack on the town and by the evening Blücher had surrendered. M. Pingaud writes that at Lübeck Bernadotte 'displayed once more all his brilliant ardour of former days'.

In a despatch of 8 November to Napoleon, he expressed his pleasure at having been able to satisfy the Emperor's expectations, and sent the enemy's standards which he had captured when the Prussians had surrendered. He received a reply which showed that the past had been, at least temporarily, forgiven if not forgotten. 'My cousin,' Napoleon wrote, 'I have received the standards which you sent me. I have observed with pleasure the activity and talents which you have displayed in the course of recent events and the distinguished valour of your troops. I testify to you my satisfaction and you can count upon my gratitude.'[5]

Bernadotte as usual earned the gratitude of the local inhabitants when he occupied Lübeck for the way they were treated by the troops and the firm steps which he took to prevent pillaging. He made such an impression that some thirty years later, at a banquet given in Lübeck for the Swedish Chargé d'Affaires, the Burgomaster said: 'This is the anniversary of the day upon which, thirty years ago, the Prince of Ponte Corvo preserved our city from pillage and from the horrors of war.'[6]

CHAPTER SEVENTEEN

Poland and Russia

The war with Prussia was now over but it was not long before Bernadotte was on the move again. Austria had been defeated in 1805 and Prussia in 1806; now it was Russia's turn which led to what is known as the Polish Campaign.[1]

When the Russians first received the news of Jena and the surrender of Blücher at Lübeck their reaction was pleasure and relief because Prussia was their most-feared enemy, but it was not long before a more realistic view was taken. As Napoleon had, temporarily at least, dealt with Austria and Prussia and it was now quite clear that his object was to conquer the whole of Europe, it would not be long, the Russians realised, before the Grand Army was ordered to invade their country.

Meanwhile Bernadotte on 8 December joined Napoleon in Posen, which was then in that part of Poland which belonged to the Prussians. By this time, fortunately, Bernadotte's faux pas on the eve of the Battle of Jena had been forgotten, largely because Napoleon had been greatly impressed by his rapid pursuit of the Prussians after Jena and his capture of Halle and Lübeck. Napoleon made it quite clear that he now had complete confidence in Bernadotte as a commander when he appointed him to lead the left wing of the Grand Army with two other Marshals, Ney and Bessières, subordinate to him. In his *Napoleon's Campaign in Poland*, F. L. Petre described Bernadotte as, 'calm, selfish, calculating and astute, of much more polished manners than most of Napoleon's marshals. He was endowed with considerable powers of command. Him the Emperor could, so far as ability was concerned, trust in a semi-independent command.'

The general advance on Warsaw began on 10 December. Bernadotte's orders were to separate the Prussians from their allies and drive them back to Koenigsberg. The weather conditions were appalling, snow and ice everywhere. The Duke of Fezensac, who was on the staff of Marshal Ney, arrived at Bernadotte's headquarters on Christmas Eve to deliver an urgent despatch and in his memoirs he wrote an interesting account of the impression which the marshal made on him.

> 'It was the only occasion that I ever met the future King of Sweden, who seemed to me very different from our other generals. In the first place he was perfectly amiable to everyone. That was the first difference. He was particularly so to me although he only knew me by name. He messed with his aides-de-camp and with other officers like myself who were on a mission. My horse was very tired, so he gave me another to ride with him. When I left him in the evening the weather was awful. I said with a laugh that I would try and not drop his despatch in the snow. He offered to keep me until the morning and to explain to Marshal Ney in a postscript to the despatch that he had done so. I thanked him but said that I must not lose a minute in returning to my post. He had passed the evening questioning the man at whose house he was lodged about the conditions of the country and the customs of the people. I feel sure that he had some hope that they would think of him in Poland (i.e. for the Throne); and

he was seeking to procure information which might be useful to him, as well as to make partisans and friends everywhere.'

The weather by this time was so bad that Bernadotte decided at the beginning of January 1807 to stop somewhere on the Baltic coast but he was not allowed to remain there for long as the Russians under General Bennigsen advanced in order to separate the left wing of the Grand Army from the remainder. They succeeded in capturing a small force of 200 which was garrisoned in Liebstadt and then advanced towards Mohrungen where there was another French outpost. As soon as the news reached Bernadotte he took immediate steps to stop the rout, as otherwise the whole of the Grand Army's left wing might have been defeated and would probably have been involved in a general retreat, the consequences of which can only be guessed.

> 'What was most remarkable [Napoleon wrote later,] was not only the bravery of the troops themselves and the skill of the generals but the rapidity with which all the corps broke up their camps and carried out a light march, which would have tried any other troops severely, without having a single man missing when the battlefield was reached. That was an achievement characteristic of soldiers who obey no motive except that of honour.'[2]

Once more another success by Bernadotte had done much to counteract the unfortunate incident when he failed to arrive in time to take part in the battle of Jena. At the same time as Bernadotte began his march he informed his two subordinate generals, Dupont and Drouet, of the situation and ordered them to march on Mohrungen. The battle was a fierce one and for a time Bernadotte's troops were out-numbered and having a difficult time. Fortunately General Dupont arrived just in time to reinforce Bernadotte and an attack by both together won the day. The Russians had to retreat but it had been a near thing and the French suffered a considerable number of casualties.

By a strange co-incidence General Bennigsen had been born in Hanover where Bernadotte was held in good repute and he returned some of Bernadotte's personal possession, which had been taken by Cossacks of the Russian army, with the following letter: 'I owe this act of courtesy to the paternal manner in which Marshal Bernadotte treated Hanover, my native country, during the time that he commanded in that place.'[3]

The Battle of Mohrungen has generally been considered his greatest performance on the battlefield during his active service as a marshal, and several historians have commented on it and compared it with other occasions when he was not acting on his own but under a superior commander. Perhaps the most acute of all these comments was made by General Zurlinden, 'all constraint over-excited his ambitious self-centred nature. He was naturally suited for an absolute command.'[4]

Less than a month later another important battle took place at Eylau which cost a lot of casualties and achieved nothing. Once again Bernadotte took no part, but on this occasion he was in no way to blame. His absence was caused by what certainly appears to have been the negligence of Napoleon's Chief of Staff—still Marshal Berthier—who entrusted orders for delivery to Bernadotte to some young officers who had only just arrived from the French Military Academy. While en route to Strasbourg, where Bernadotte was at the moment, they were taken prisoner by Cossacks.

Bernadotte was in no way responsible and when another

order reached him which referred to the earlier despatch he wrote to Berthier:

> 'The orders you inform me were sent on the 31st have never reached me. The bearers were taken prisoners at Lautenberg. They were young officers from the Military School. As I do not know the contents of your Orders of the 31st I am not sure whether my movement towards Kauernick accords with the Emperor's wishes.... I am afraid that the despatches intercepted by the enemy may have been very useful to them by making them hasten their retreat.
>
> Marshal Bernadotte,
> Prince of Ponte Corvo.'[5]

Napoleon, to do him justice, although he liked to seize any opportunity that arose to criticise his 'Cousin', once he heard all the evidence on this particular occasion did all he could to let it be known that he still had complete confidence in his marshal. In one of the letters which he wrote to Bernadotte after the Eylau incident he made this quite clear. 'I have learned with pleasure,' he wrote, 'that you are satisfied with the spirit displayed by your troops. It is enough if you can communicate to them that love of glory and that zeal for the honour of my Army by which you yourself are inspired.'[6]

Nothing very important happened during the next three months until 4 June when a minor operation took place at Spandau, on the bank of the river Passarge, and during which Bernadotte was wounded. Immediately she heard the news his wife Désirée left Paris for Poland and looked after him for six weeks until he had fully recovered.

While he was still being nursed by his wife he received a letter from Juliette Récamier in which she said how much she had missed hearing from him for the past two years. His reply was as follows:

> 'That I am far from deserving your reproaches General Junot will be my witness. On the night before Austerlitz I left him at eleven o'clock after assuring him that on my return to my bivouac I would write to you. He gave me a thousand messages for you. With my head and my heart absorbed in your troubles, I expressed to you all the pain which your reverse of fortune had caused me. I was speaking to you and occupied with you on the eve of that day which was to decide the destiny of the world. My letter was committed to the post, and should have reached you. When friendship, tenderness and susceptibility inflame the heart everything that is expressed is deeply felt. I have never ceased to address to you my hopes and good wishes and, although fated to be ever your devoted servant, I do not wish to weary you with my letters. Farewell. If you still think of me believe me that you are my chief ideal and that nothing can equal the tender and affectionate sentiments which I have dedicated to your worship.'[7]

Before Bernadotte had fully recovered from his wounds the Polish campaign had ended, Napoleon having defeated the Russo-Prussian forces on 15 June 1807 at Friedland, as a result of which the Treaty of Tilsit was signed between Napoleon and the Emperor Alexander of Russia. One of the main clauses of the treaty was an agreement, very much against Alexander's will, that he would join with France in an effort to blockade all British trade from entering the Baltic Sea or any of the ports of northern Germany.

It was because of this latter condition, namely the blocking of the northern German ports, that Bernadotte was made responsible for the occupation of the three Hanseatic cities,

Hamburg, Bremen and Lübeck, and appointed governor. These three cities were of course the three most important ports close to the mouths of the Elbe, Weser and Trave rivers. As Sir Plunket Barton wrote, 'if Venice is entitled to be called Queen of the Adriatic, these three Hanseatic cities might fitly have been decribed as the three Sovereign Princesses of the Northern Seas'. They were determined to remain politically independent and considered that they had every reason to be so because of their commercial importance. Even at that time they were doing a very prosperous trade with England, and the so-called continental system which had been introduced by Napoleon in 1806 to stifle it was already beginning to do so to an alarming extent.

When Bernadotte arrived in Hamburg on 23 July to take up his new appointment he was already well aware that it was not going to be easy. It had already been made clear to him, before he was sent there by Napoleon, that if as a result of the Treaty of Tilsit, England would not make peace with France and Russia, then Denmark, Sweden, Portugal and Austria would be called upon to close their ports to all British trade and also to declare war upon her. Furthermore if Sweden refused to do this Denmark would be asked to declare war upon Sweden. This was confirmed in a letter written to Bernadotte by Napoleon: 'If England refuses to accept the Russian mediation Denmark must declare war against her or I must declare war on Denmark. In the latter event your duty will be to seize the whole Danish continent. You must make a great fuss about Denmark having opened the passage of the Sound, and having allowed their seas to be invaded, which to the Danes ought to be as inviolable as their territory itself.'[8]

The mention by Napoleon of the Danes 'having opened the passage of the Sound' was very soon to have vital repercussions. This part of Napoleon's letter was a reference to a British expedition which had recently entered the Sound but eventually returned to England without taking any action. It had been sent there by Canning and its only object, apparently, was to make it clear to the Danes that if the British wanted to invade Denmark they would find little difficulty in doing so. Bernadotte's immediate reaction to Napoleon's letter was to advise him to capture Copenhagen and close the Sound. Napoleon, however, did not do so and by this time Canning, having realised the situation, took immediate action to forestall any attack on Denmark by the French and Russians by bombarding Copenhagen and capturing the Danish fleet.

When Copenhagen surrendered it was occupied by the British for about six weeks which resulted in the King of Denmark sending an envoy to visit Bernadotte in Hamburg to ask for help from France should British occupation continue. This led to the signing of the Treaty of Fontainebleau between France and Denmark on 31 October, by which it was agreed that, should it be necessary, Bernadotte's army would occupy Denmark and defend it in the event of a British invasion. Nothing happened until March 1808, because Napoleon had his hands full in Italy, but even after his return to Paris he marked time because he was not particularly interested in Denmark and was not anxious to take over the responsibility of the defence of the Danes unless they were prepared to provide at least 13,000 of the necessary garrison. Before the end of March, however, something else was to take place which once again temporarily took Napoleon's attention from Denmark. It happened that there was under Bernadotte's command a Spanish force about 14,000 strong and it was not surprising that they got on well together. He understood them and he was very popular with them.

They knew he was a Béarnais and he spoke reasonably good Spanish.

On 18 March 1808 after a revolution in the north-east of Spain Charles IX abdicated in favour of his son Ferdinand. At this moment Napoleon stepped in since he saw the situation as an opportunity to get one of his family on the throne. His brother Louis refused it and so did Joseph at first, because he did not want to leave Naples, though later on he decided to accept. In the meantime, however, Napoleon had actually sent someone to inform Bernadotte that he might be given command of the French armies in Spain with the prospect of becoming King of Spain and the Balearic Isles. It was thought by Napoleon that his marshal might quite probably accept the Spanish command because he had frequently complained about not having French troops under his command. It was then that Bernadotte told his friend Madame de Staël that he had no wish to become King of the Balearic Isles and that in any event Napoleon could not make him King of Spain, but that if he were given orders by the Emperor to command the Spanish Army he would naturally obey.[9]

When Joseph Bonaparte did accept the offer it was rather embarrassing for Bernadotte, who was still commanding the Spanish forces in the Grand Army, because he had to require them to swear allegiance to his brother-in-law. They did this without much argument, but only because they did not know the truth about their king's abdication, nor had they any idea that it was a revolution which had caused it. When they did learn all the facts they were soon in a state of mutiny. Nine thousand of them, under their commander the Marquis de la Romana and with the help of a British admiral, managed to embark at Copenhagen and return to Spain. The remainder were unable to get away and Napoleon had them all arrested and imprisoned in France.

CHAPTER EIGHTEEN

The Hanseatic Towns

There was only another year and nine months to run before Bernadotte left the Hanseatic Towns, and having regard to the fact that by the end of October 1810 he was to become Crown Prince of Sweden it is interesting to consider some of the comments which have been made about the way in which he carried out his duties as governor.

General Zurlinden in his *Napoleon and his Marshals* stated that amongst other things the governor had to deal with Sweden and 'he behaved with so much moderation, justice and skill as to win the affection of that country'. Bernard Sarrans in his *History of Bernadotte* wrote: 'Nobody possessed in such a high degree as Bernadotte the talent for creating order out of disorder, for giving dignity to coercion, for winning the gratitude of the peoples of whom he was appointed the oppressor.' Finally Bourrienne, who was French Minister in Hamburg, said that by the favourable impression which he left behind him in that city he unconsciously paved his way to the Swedish throne.

A well-known Danish diplomat who was in Hamburg from 1811 until 1813 wrote about Bernadotte's reputation in Hanover, in a book of reminiscences published in 1884. His name was Rist and he met Bernadotte when he was in Hamburg as Danish Consul-General. During his diplomatic career he had also personally known Napoleon, Czar Alexander—who was later to become a friend and admirer of

Bernadotte—Wellington and Blücher. The following is a translation of Rist's description of Bernadotte as he knew him.

'Immediately after my arrival in Hamburg I called on the Prince de Ponte Corvo, Commander-in-Chief of the French forces there, better known as Marshal Bernadotte, who had his headquarters at Baron Voght's beautiful house in Flottbeck. Whatever I might have heard about the French marshal's way of life, I have rarely met a more impressive figure at least as regards his outward appearance. A well-proportioned body, a fine and noble poise, pronounced but nevertheless attractive features, his accent and talkativeness, so characteristic of people from Southern France, combined with his good nature, have made him popular both with troops and with foreigners. Because of his kindness he was highly appreciated in Hanover where he was in command of the occupation force for quite a long time.'

Rist compared him with Marshal Davout, who was no friend of Bernadotte and whom Rist called 'Napoleon's blind tool and favourite ... who after the establishment of the Confederation of the Rhine, with an iron hand and all the hated paraphernalia of spies, gendarmes, censorship and military courts, tried to oppress Germans and German mentality in Southern Germany.'

It was shortly before he was to leave the Hanseatic Towns that he heard of the death of his mother, of whom he was very fond. She died where he was born, in the town of Pau. He immediately wrote to his brother:

'My dear Brother, I have received with profound grief the news of the loss we have sustained by the death of our beloved and revered mother. I was so little prepared for this sad event that I was cherishing the hope of soon being able to pay a visit to Pau for the purpose of seeing her and of folding her in my arms. Providence has decided otherwise and we must submit to its decrees although the pain caused by such a great and sudden loss is cruel indeed. I thank you, my dear brother, for your consolatory words. I appreciate their sincerity and receive them with gratitude. Farewell, my dear brother. Preserve your health for the sake of your wife and children and believe me that I am as inseparably bound to you.

Your brother, J. Bernadotte.

'P.S. I beg of you to convey to the magisterial body of the public officers of Pau my grateful recognition of the touching proof of their attachment which they have displayed towards me on the occasion of this sad event.'[1]

It was while he was stationed at Dresden in March 1809 waiting to receive orders from Napoleon for a new campaign that was being planned that Bernadotte heard about the revolution in Sweden when Gustavus IV was deposed and his uncle, the Duke of Sudermenia, appointed Regent. Once again he was able to gain praise and admiration from the Swedes who approached him shortly after the revolution asking for an armistice, which he granted them. According to the British Ambassador in Stockholm, who sent a report to the British Foreign Office about it, Bernadotte gave the envoy who was sent by the Regent of Sweden to ask for the armistice 'a most favourable and flattering reception'.[2]

Bourrienne in his *L'Histoire Générale* wrote that some people suspected that Bernadotte was 'playing up' to his future subjects, but this is extremely unlikely. Bourrienne also said that Bernadotte once told him that a fortune-teller had prophesied that he would 'cross the sea to become a King' which might have been the cause of the suspicion on the part of those who knew of the prophesy.

While Bernadotte had been in Hanover Napoleon had begun to make it inevitable that he would come to a disastrous end, and cracks in the fabric of the French Empire were already becoming visible. The capitulation of about 23,000 troops in Baylen on 19 July 1808, called by Napoleon himself 'The Blunder of Bayonne', made it clear that the new Spain had become a force in Europe which would greatly assist in the gradual downfall of Napoleon. It greatly encouraged Austria which was now determined to make some effort to avenge its defeat at Austerlitz.

On 10 April the Austrians invaded Bavaria without any formal declaration of war, described in the *Cambridge Modern History* as 'the starting point of the popular reaction against the despotism of Napoleon'. There were also other difficulties which have been described in Albert Sorel's *L'Europe et la Revolution française*. It did not matter where Napoleon was, something was going wrong all the time. When he left his armies to go to Paris they usually suffered a defeat and when he left Paris to return to the battlefield Fouché always expected that there was going to be a coup d'état.

After Bernadotte had been in Dresden for nearly three weeks vainly waiting for orders from the Emperor, he wrote a very strong letter to Napoleon stating that all he had received was a reprimand from General Berthier. It was not the first time that this had happened and he was beginning to suspect that it had been done deliberately. He had been informed however that he had been appointed to command the Saxon army, and this he did not want. This letter is quoted almost in full because of its importance in making quite clear that he was at this time convinced that he was a victim of Napoleon's dislike; and it also explains why three months later he became involved in one of the most unpleasant events in his whole career.

'Sire, today 11 April I have received from Headquarters the first despatches that have reached me since my arrival in Dresden. . . . The Major-General [Berthier, the Chief of Staff] complains of not having received from me a report on the situation of the Polish Army, General Dupas' division and General Bruyère's brigade. I have the honour to represent to your Majesty that Berthier's message informs me for the first time that the Polish Army and the French troops in Hanover form part of the new command which your Majesty has assigned me when summoning me to Dresden. It was all the more impossible for me to guess your Majesty's intention, since I learned yesterday by chance that General Dupas' division has left Hanover in obedience to an order coming directly from the Major-General. I say nothing of the distance which separates me from these Corps. I have already had the honour of entreating Your Majesty to relieve me of the command of the Saxons. I have already explained to Your Majesty that I feel unequal to the task of leading foreigners. I eagerly await Your Majesty's kind assent to my prayer; for the treatment which I experience every day affects my morale very sensibly and exhausts all the energies of my soul. I came to Dresden without having received any instructions. The first letter containing orders, which by the hazards of war might have been of the utmost importance, has been sent to me by post and took sixteen days to reach me. All this, Sire, makes me tremble for the success of my operations; when I see my efforts perpetually paralysed by a hidden force over which I cannot prevail. I implore Your Majesty to grant me my retirement, unless you will deign to employ me in some distant expedition, where my enemies would no longer be interested in persecuting me.

J. B. Bernadotte
Prince of Ponte Corvo.'[3]

Two further letters were written in the absence of a reply but on 29 April Napoleon sent the following letter which made no reference whatsoever to the complaints which Bernadotte had made.

'My Cousin, I have received all your letters. In the war which I am entering I am supported by Russia and you are marked out for something in that connection. Accordingly you will receive the command which I have assigned to you as a mark of my esteem and regard.

Napoleon.'[4]

The reason why Bernadotte was almost always given command of foreign troops rather than French has been given in an English book about Napoleon's Marshals. 'Napoleon always took care that Bernadotte should never have under his command French soldiers. His troops in 1805 were Bavarians, in 1807 Poles, in 1808 Dutch and Spaniards and in 1809 Poles and Saxons. Berthier working out the Emperor's ideas, and himself hating Bernadotte, took care that in the allotment of duties the disagreeable and unimportant tasks should fall on the Marshal.'[5]

CHAPTER NINETEEN

The Campaign of 1809

In 1809 Napoleon began the most important campaign he had conducted since the beginning of the Empire. Between 13 April and 12 May he had advanced from the Danube as far as Ratisbon and captured en route about 50,000 prisoners and 100 guns.

While in Ratisbon Napoleon ordered Bernadotte to leave Dresden and an announcement was made that he would march through Bohemia. This resulted in the Austrians leaving some of their troops in Bohemia to attack Bernadotte when he arrived, which enabled Napoleon to enter Vienna with practically no opposition.

Unfortunately at about the same time the Grand Army met with a very serious defeat at Essling, suffering severe losses including the death of Marshal Lannes. Coming at this particular time it caused much doubt about the future of the French Emperor and there were rumours that Fouché was wondering whether in the near future Bernadotte might become Napoleon's successor. According to Pelet there was a strong feeling among many Frenchmen that Napoleon's military ambition might lead to national disaster, and there were many people in France of some importance who were seriously considering whether there was not somebody who could succeed as head of revolutionary France without endangering her position in Europe where she already had so many enemies.

Nevertheless, Napoleon very soon wrote to Bernadotte informing him that he expected to get reinforcements of about 60,000 from his Italian army. This good news enabled Napoleon to prepare for a new campaign which culminated in the battle of Wagram—an unfortunate battle in so far as Bernadotte was concerned, although it was a victory for Napoleon. Bernadotte displayed as usual great bravery but as Leonce Pingaud wrote 'at Wagram everything contributed to make him a defeated general in a victorious army: his yielding to discouragement, the slowness of his movements and the bad quality of his troops.... His Saxon troops failed again. He exposed himself bravely in order to rally them against the attacking force. Seven or eight of his staff were killed or wounded, and he had a narrow escape from death from a sword-thrust. Napoleon came in person and helped to inspire some of his battalions.'[1]

There is no doubt that Napoleon and Bernadotte had an open quarrel on the field of battle but what made it worse was an Order of the Day which Bernadotte issued afterwards. When reading it one should remember that on several occasions he had told Napoleon, and also put it in writing, that his Saxon troops were unreliable. The Order of the Day, which was dated 9 July—i.e. four days after the battle—was as follows:

> 'Saxons, on the day of 5 July, between 7,000 and 8,000 of you pierced the centre of the enemy's army and fought your way to the Deutch–Wagram in spite of the resistance of 40,000 of the enemy supported by 50 guns. You fought until midnight and you bivouacked in the middle of the Austrian lines. On the 6th at daybreak you renewed the combat with the same perseverance. Amidst the ravages of the enemy's artillery your living columns remained as

motionless as bronze. The great Napoleon witnessed your devotion. He numbers you among his braves. Saxons, a soldier's fortune consists in doing his duty: you have nobly done yours.'[2]

Some of the Order of the Day was not untrue, some was misleading and some of it, such as the statement that the Saxons under artillery fire remained 'as motionless as bronze', was completely untrue. Napoleon and the other marshals who took part in the battle would probably not have taken any action if the Order had not been published in a Frankfort newspaper.

Three weeks later Napoleon wrote the following letter to the Minister of War.

'If you have an occasion to see the Prince of Ponte Corvo please convey to him my displeasure at the ridiculous Order of the Day which he has published in all the newspapers. It is all the more out of place because he himself was complaining about the Saxons during the whole day. The Order of the Day contains other inaccuracies. It was General Oudinot who took Wagram on 6 July at mid-day: so the Prince of Ponte Corvo could not have taken it. It is not true that the Saxons forced the enemy's centre on the 5th. They did not fire a shot. Speaking generally I shall be well pleased that you should know that the Prince of Ponte Corvo has not done well in this campaign. He is a man who wants riches, pleasures and greatness but does not wish to buy them by the dangers and fatigues of war. In truth that column of bronze was constantly routed.

Napoleon.'[3]

When the ridiculous Order of the Day, as Napoleon called it, had first been brought to his notice, he allowed Bernadotte to leave the army. The strange explanation was to permit him to 'take the waters' at Plombiers-les-Bains in the Vosges. He did not go there but returned to his country house where he remained until shortly after the occupation of the island of Walcheren which was regarded as a national crisis.

It was decided, after a lot of argument, to call up the reserves and it was suggested that Bernadotte should be appointed to command them under the title of Commander-in-Chief of the Army of Defence. This again caused a good deal of trouble as the Minister of War was not willing to make such an appointment without the personal approval of the Emperor. Fortunately before the middle of August Napoleon gave his instructions for Bernadotte to become Commander-in-Chief of the newly formed army which he named the Army of Antwerp.[4]

The main object of what is known as the Walcheren Expedition was to destroy the naval base at Antwerp, one of the bases from which Napoleon would launch any invasion of the British Isles. The expedition failed mainly because of the British decision to occupy the island of Walcheren. Sir Plunket Barton, in *Bernadotte and Napoleon*, described what happened on the island and the repercussions of the disaster.

> 'The British military authorities were unaware of the climate of Walcheren. It was a place where the natives lived in a chronic state of fever and ague while it was a positive death-trap to strangers. The sickness and mortality in the camp was terrible. The principal occupation of the troops was burying the dead; while in the hospitals there were 4,000 before the end of August and 10,000 before the end of September. On 21 September a small fever-stricken remnant of the once magnificent army re-embarked and

returned to England. The aftermath of the expedition entailed the court-martial of the commander, a duel between Castlereagh and Canning and a ministerial crisis as a result of which Perceval became Premier.'

Meanwhile from the moment that Bernadotte was appointed to command the Army of Antwerp he made the necessary arrangements for the defence of the naval base and had the attack ever taken place it would have met with considerable resistance. What the outcome would have been no one can say because fever and ague did the job for him.

The only pleasant thing about it all is a story told by M. de Rocca in his account of the disastrous expedition. Bernadotte when inspecting the various defence outposts on the outskirts of Antwerp 'stopped at a cottage and was given a cup of milk by an old woman who, like most of the country people, disliked French rule. He rewarded her with a gold coin. She looked at it with glad surprise and exclaimed: "The English have come at last. That's a good job."'[5]

CHAPTER TWENTY

Napoleon versus Bonaparte

The next three months were unpleasant for Bernadotte because Napoleon had again taken umbrage at one of the Marshal's Orders of the Day, in which he thought there was an implication by Bernadotte that Napoleon had only provided him with 15,000 men for the defence of Antwerp. Because of this he wrote a letter to the Minister of War:

> 'My intention is not to leave the command in the hands of the Prince of Ponte Corvo who continues to correspond with the intriguers of Paris and who is a man in whom I can no longer place confidence. You will let him know that I disapprove of his Order of the Day, that it is not true that he has only 15,000 men since with the Corps of the Duke of Coneglians [Marshal Moncey] and with that of the Duke of Istria [Marshal Bessières] I have on the Scheldt 60,000 men. But even if he had only 15,000 men his duty was to conceal that from the enemy; this is the first occasion on which a General has been known to betray his position by an excess of his vanity'.[1]

On the same day Napoleon wrote to Fouché, by now Duke of Otranto, that he had already given the Minister of War orders to recall Bernadotte with whom he was 'highly displeased'. 'His talent,' he wrote, 'is very mediocre. I have no kind of faith in him. He lends a willing ear to all the intriguers who inundate the great capital ...'

This letter was followed up by another written the following day which contained, in addition to a number of unjustified suspicions, several untruths and malevolent suggestions. This letter is quoted in full:

> 'The Prince of Ponte Corvo who is going to Paris will probably have a conversation with you. You will let him know that I was displeased with his Order of the Day to the Saxons which had a tendency to ascribe glory to them which was not their due, for they were in flight during the whole of the 6th; that I have not been less displeased with his Order of the Day to the National Guard in which he says he had only 15,000 men, whereas I had 60,000 on the Scheldt; that even if he had only 10,000 it is a criminal act on a General's part to let the enemy and all Europe into the secret of his numerical strength; that he has no sense of proportion; that I was very much dissatisfied during the Swedish business at his having allowed the Swedes admission to our ports provisionally, thus compromising me with Russia; that he receives letters from a party of schemers in Paris; that I know he is not fool enough to listen to them but that the thing itself is improper; that I cannot endure intrigues; that it is both his duty and interest to be straight-forward; that he must get rid of all this rabble and not permit them to write to him; and that if he does not, misfortune will overtake him. The Prince of Ponte Corvo made a great deal of money at Hamburg. He made money too at Elbing. That brought the bad business in Poland and the battle of Eylau on me. I am tired of schemes and I am shocked that a man whom I have loaded with benefits should lend his ear to a set of wretches whom he knows and values at their proper worth. You will tell him that he has never seen a man nor received a

letter without my knowledge; that I am aware how little importance he attaches to it all, but to permit such men to write to him and to receive them is to encourage them. All this is private and confidential. You will make no use of these details unless the Prince of Ponte Corvo should speak to you. If he does not, you will not say anything to him.

Napoleon.'

When Bernadotte arrived back in Paris from Antwerp the Minister of War, more or less in accordance with Napoleon's instructions, told the Marshal that the Emperor wanted him to pay a visit to Ponte Corvo, but he refused and said that rather than obey such an order he was prepared to disclaim all his titles and retire.

When Napoleon was told this he had to try and think of some other way of getting rid of Bernadotte from Paris, where he thought the schemers would be dangerous. Finally he decided, thinking that it would tempt Bernadotte, to appoint him as the representative of France in the Holy City with the title of Governor-General. When Bernadotte refused the offer and again said that all he wanted to do was to retire Napoleon wrote him another persuasive letter.[2]

'You have indeed won enough glory [he wrote] to justify you in seeking repose. I do not know why it is, but I see very well that we do not understand each other. My policy, however, requires that you should go to Rome and hold my court there. You will have a great position. I have assigned you two millions for your expenses as Governor-General, I only ask you to remain there for eighteen months. We shall have no more direct relations with each other. Perhaps you will change your ideas.'

Bernadotte was still most reluctant to accept the appointment, but fortunately, something happened which made Napoleon change his mind. For some reason it became necessary in May 1810 to get rid of Fouché as Minister of Police, and he was offered and accepted the appointment of Governor-General of Rome. Fortunate it was, for the whole of Bernadotte's future was shortly going to change in a most unexpected way.

CHAPTER TWENTY-ONE

The Throne of Sweden

On 2 June 1810 the King of Sweden wrote the following letter to Napoleon:

'My brother and Cousin,

'Both I and my Kingdom have just sustained the most terrible of blows through the unexpected death of my beloved son, H.R.H. the Prince Royal of Sweden. He had by his rare qualities won the love of my people. Sweden suddenly sees itself thrown back into a situation in which the present offers no guarantees for the future beyond the uncertain duration of my life. In whom can I better trust than in your Imperial and Royal Majesty who has so many claims upon my confidence and upon the gratitude of all good Swedes? ... I am obliged to summon the Diet to meet in July to decide the important question of the succession to the throne.... It is of great importance that I should receive a reply from your Imperial and Royal Majesty before the Diet meets. I must say frankly that my people do not wish to experience the inconvenience of a long minority, and the wishes of the Diet incline to a Prince who is of an age which renders him capable of succeeding me in the event of my death and possesses children whose existence assures the continuance of the dynasty. If, as I am glad to think, the maintenance of intimate relations between Sweden and Denmark accord with your Imperial and Royal Majesty's political views might this object not be attained by the election of the Duke of Augustenburg, brother-in-law of the King of Denmark, who has three children two of whom are sons aged twelve and ten respectively? Being a brother of the Prince whom Sweden has just lost, he will succeed him in the love of my subjects, who will see in his children a pledge of security for the future. I desire eagerly to receive the advice of your Imperial and Royal Majesty on that point and I rejoice to think that you will not in such a critical moment abandon a loyal and generous nation, attached to France by sympathy and affection which counts confidently on your Imperial and Royal Majesty's support and is ready to sacrifice anything except her independence, her traditions and her laws.

Charles, King of Sweden'

After discussing the above letter with the Swedish ambassador in Paris, at his request, Napoleon eventually agreed that probably the best solution would be the Duke of Augustenburg who was married to a sister of the King of Denmark. Nevertheless the Emperor was not in the least bit interested in the Swedish succession and all he did was to send a noncommital reply to the king.

Meanwhile in Sweden there was no enthusiasm for having Augustenburg as the heir to the Swedish throne. Count Ferson, when told of the Prince Royal's death, is reported to have said, 'Sweden is lost unless we choose one of Napoleon's Marshals.' It was perfectly true that during the reign of Gustavus IV Sweden had deteriorated enormously and the Russian Chancellor had described the country as being 'in the agony of death and nothing remains but to let her die in peace'.*

* See *Bernadotte and Napoleon* by Sir Plunket Barton.

The Swedes knew a great deal about Bernadotte and had personal experience of him when he had been Governor of Hanover and the Hanseatic Towns and particularly after the capture of Lübeck when he had treated the local inhabitants and his Swedish prisoners of war with clemency. A Swede who admired Bernadotte very much was Count Gustave Mörner, who had been in command of the Swedes taken prisoner at Lübeck. The Count expressed the view that in the difficulty in which Sweden found herself after the death of the heir apparent, the best way out would be to choose a French general, for example the Prince of Ponte Corvo.

A young relation of Baron Mörner had, as King's Messenger, delivered to Napoleon the letter from his King quoted above and he remained in Paris for some time before returning to Sweden. While he was there he became very interested in the suggestion that Bernadotte might be an excellent choice for election as Prince Royal of Sweden and made a lot of inquiries. He was very impressed by the fact that not only was Bernadotte an efficient soldier and a good administrator but he was also related by marriage to the Emperor of France. Having confirmed these facts he succeeded in obtaining an interview with the Marshal which he followed up with the following letter:[1]

Paris 25 June 1810

'My Prince,

Your modesty cannot shake my opinion which I believe will be that of the wisest of my compatriots. Sweden does not need a Dane, or a Russian or a boy whose minority would do us an injury. These are the lines on which I shall speak whether it be to my Sovereign or to the Diet. I shall declare both to one and to the other that our country requires a Frenchman who will adopt our religion, who is known for his talents, for his courage and for the esteem in which he is held by the august Emperor of France, who belongs to the Emperor's family, being brother-in-law to the King of Spain; who has a son who will be able to replace his father without a regency when Providence so ordains. I do not think that I am mistaken in anticipating that this view will be generally adopted, unless your great Emperor has other intentions as regards your future. But if his wishes accord with those of the great majority of Swedes and those of the Army, he will render them a service which will place them under a lasting obligation to him. At all events nothing will prevent me from expressing my own personal opinion to the Diet; and whatever may result I shall have the satisfaction of having done my duty, and of having no other object in view than to serve my country and to render a just homage to your merits. I am, with the most profound respect, your Highness's very humble and obedient servant,

Baron Otto Mörner'

At the interview which Mörner had with him before the letter was written, Bernadotte had made one thing clear—namely, that if he were approached he would not accept the offer without first obtaining his Emperor's approval and being satisfied that the present King of Sweden was really in favour of his becoming Crown Prince. Although Bernadotte was to be elected heir apparent before the year was out, there was quite a lot of argument to take place before the final decision was made. Moreover young Mörner was to get into trouble for what the Swedish ambassador called 'the extreme irregularity' of his interview with Bernadotte. On his return to Sweden he was arrested but very soon released and ordered to go back and rejoin his regiment.

When this news reached Bernadotte he was most upset and wrote the following letter to Mörner:[2]

> 'I have heard with much pain, Baron, of the annoyances to which you have been subjected on my account. I feel too much concerned not to take every means in my power of putting an end to them. Be persuaded that I shall lose no opportunity of proving to you the sincerity of the sentiments with which I shall always remain, Baron, your affectionate friend.
>
> J. Bernadotte,
> Prince of Ponte Corvo'

The reason why the Swedish ambassador in Paris wrote a very strong letter to his Foreign Secretary in Stockholm was because he knew nothing about what had been going on between Baron Mörner and Bernadotte until about three days after it had happened, but it is interesting to note that in spite of his annoyance he included the following in his letter: 'the extreme irregularity of the proceedings which have put him (Bernadotte) forward does not prevent me saying that he is a Prince highly to be commended for his excellent qualities, his talents, his valour, and his experience. He enjoys in this country general regard and esteem.'

Although Napoleon's experiences had rather disillusioned him over attempts to impose a king on a people without any regard for his suitability, he became quite intrigued when he realised that there was a fairly strong desire on the part of the Swedes to have a Frenchman as their king. Nevertheless he was not at first impressed with the Swedes' interest in Bernadotte, but whether this was for personal reasons or because he was not aware of the strength of Bernadotte's reputation it is not possible to say.

There is, however, some evidence contained in a despatch

of 9 July 1810 by Metternich that Napoleon was considering transferring Murat from Naples to Sweden, his brother Jerome from Westphalia to Naples and his other brother Louis from Holland to Westphalia.[3] Some of the Bonaparte family, however, did not like the idea of having to change their religion as would have been necessary, but it did not worry Bernadotte who had reminded Mörner that he had been born in Pau, the birthplace of Henry of Navarre who became Henry IV. He was supposed to have said that Paris was worth a mass and had become a Roman Catholic, and Bernadotte was perfectly prepared to do the opposite.[4] Eventually, however, Napoleon came round to supporting the candidature of Bernadotte and on 21 July formally told his Marshal that he was in favour of his becoming heir to the throne of Sweden.

This took place during a levée held by the Emperor when Napoleon asked Bernadotte whether he had any news from Sweden. Bernadotte did not answer but asked the Emperor to tell him whether his election to the Swedish succession could be consistent with his Imperial Majesty's policy. If it were not then he would prevent any further steps being taken to bring it about. The Swedish ambassador, who was present at the levée, in a despatch written on 22 August, gave the Emperor's reply. 'Do nothing of the kind. Let things take their course. It is consistent with my policy and with that of Sweden that you should be placed there.'

King Charles XIII of Sweden, however, still wanted his cousin the Duke of Augustenburg to be elected but apparently a majority of the Diet were for the Prince of Ponte Corvo, and a large section of that majority were the ordinary members who were attracted by Bernadotte's military career and personality.

Count Wrede, who had also had a meeting with Bernadotte in Paris just after Baron Mörner, expressed in the following letter his own view of the candidate for Sweden's throne which was shared by a large number of other Swedes. The letter was sent to the Duke of Oldenburg who was also a candidate but who had no chance of being elected whatsoever.

> 'Do you wish to know my opinion of Marshal Bernadotte? [Wrede wrote] I entertain for him a profound esteem not only as a soldier and statesman, but as a private individual. Vox populi Dei. Good father, good husband, faithful in his friendships, he is adored by those who form his entourage. A certain independence of character is probably the cause of the rumours of his disagreements with the Emperor. I have often seen them together without ever remarking anything of the kind. Everybody knows the regard which Napoleon has for him. He is the only real Frenchman I have found in Paris, for the others have the German air, which is stiff and disagreeable. To raise to the throne of Sweden a prince without force of character and eminent qualities would be to degrade Sweden from the ranks of an independent nation.'[5]

Until 21 August, however, there was still opposition from the king who preferred to have as his successor a relation rather than somebody whom he described as 'a French parvenu'. What he actually said was related by his aide-de-camp Count Suremain. 'However good his qualities may be, don't you realise the absurdity of my taking a French corporal as the heir to my throne?'[6]

On the 21 August the Diet voted on the matter and their decision was reported to the Swedish ambassador in Paris in the following letter from Baron d'Engeström:

> 'His Majesty has always rendered justice to the virtuous and brilliant qualities which in such an eminent degree

distinguish His Highness the Prince of Ponte Corvo; and as your despatches have convinced him that the election of the Prince will be agreeable to His Majesty the Emperor of the French, the King who desires to seize every opportunity of proving to the Emperor his friendship and devotion, has proposed to the nation the warrior who has distinguished himself in so many feats of arms under the banners of the great man who now rules the destinies of Europe.

'You know how that proposition has been received by the Diet. The decision at which they have unanimously arrived will be all the more precious in the eyes of the Prince because he will see in it the expression of the mutual confidence which unites the King and his people.'[7]

Count Gustave Mörner was given the honour and pleasure of informing Bernadotte of his election because he had been in command of the Swedish soldiers who had been taken prisoner by Bernadotte at Lübeck in 1806 and treated so well.

In the British Foreign Office papers of 1810 there is a letter written by a Swedish Minister named de Jierta from which the following is a quotation.

'The Prince, whose noble sentiments and independence of character are well known, is likely, better than anyone else, to protect our commercial interests and, with that objective in view, maintain our existing relations with England. That will be his surest way of gaining the affection of his future subjects. He will become a Swede and a good Swede, just as in Holland the brother of the Emperor became a Dutchman, and our geographical position will enable him to do so. If you add to these considerations the absolute necessity for Sweden to have a firm and vigorous Prince in order to consolidate her domestic affairs I feel that so enlightened a government as that of England will do justice to the motives of our choice.'

In Paris, on the day before the election in the Swedish Diet took place, Bernadotte had a meeting in which he made it absolutely clear to the Emperor that he 'would never consent to become King of Sweden except on conditions of complete independence'.[8]

As soon as Bernadotte had received official notice of his election as Prince Royal he wanted to be regarded as the adopted son of the present king. This was conveyed to Charles XIII by the Swedish ambassador in Paris and a few days later Bernadotte wrote his first letter to the King which, owing to its importance, is quoted in full:

> 'Sire, I shall not attempt to portray to Your Majesty the sentiments by which I have been penetrated on learning that a nation illustrious in the annals of the world has deigned to fix its eyes upon a soldier who owes all his merits to his love of country. It would be equally difficult for me to express adequately my gratitude and my admiration for the astonishing magnanimity with which Your Majesty has yourself been pleased to propose as your successor a man with whom you are connected by no tie. The idea that Your Majesty believed you were acting for the benefit of the Swedish people is one so infinitely flattering for me as to impose upon me still greater obligation. I do not disguise from myself the extent and difficulty of these obligations but I believe in my heart that I shall discharge them. Never did there exist a more powerful motive to inspire the soul of a mortal. Never was there presented to anyone such a notable opportunity of devoting his life to the happiness of a whole community. As soon as I received

Your Majesty's letter I lost no time in communicating it to His Majesty the Emperor and King. He has deigned to crown all the favours which he has conferred upon me by authorising me to become Your Majesty's adopted son. After what Your Majesty has deigned to say to me I shall hasten my departure, so as to lay at Your Majesty's feet the homage due to your virtues and to make Your Majesty the depository of my oaths of fealty. Hitherto the service of the country of my birth has been my glory and my happiness but I dare flatter myself that France will deign to applaud my efforts on behalf of my new country. She cannot fail to look with interest upon one of her sons who is summoned by the destinies of the world to defend a generous people which she has counted for a long time among her worthiest allies.

Marshal Bernadotte,
Prince of Ponte Corvo'

At the same time he wrote a letter to Napoleon informing him that the election had gone in his favour and asking the Emperor to let him know that he had the authority to accept the title of Prince Royal together with all that it involved. A reply was received informing Bernadotte that the Letters Patent had been issued authorising him to accept, but also pointing out that a special clause had been included to the effect that he could never personally bear arms against France. 'The restriction', the letter said, 'is in conformity with the constitution of the Empire....'[9]

This condition Bernadotte would not accept and he made it quite clear that unless it were struck out he could not accept the position of Prince Royal of Sweden because he would not be the vassal of a foreign country. Bernadotte fully intended to refuse the offer of Crown Prince if this clause was not withdrawn but this did not become necessary, for Napoleon finally had it deleted.

The above facts are fully supported by the contents of a despatch which was sent to King Charles XIII of Sweden by the Swedish ambassador in Paris.[10]

> 'Your Majesty knows that the completion of the Letters Patent releasing His Royal Highness from his oath of fidelity were delayed on account of the requisite formalities. There is another more serious cause of delay and Your Majesty will be pleased to hear that it has been settled most honourably. It was proposed at the Emperor's Council to follow the precedent established under Louis XIV when Philip V was placed on the throne of Spain. On that occasion a clause was inscribed in the Letters Patent binding Philip as a Frenchman by birth never to bear arms against France. The Emperor felt that, His Royal Highness the Prince Royal having been called by the free vote of the Swedish people, such a reservation would not have a good effect on Sweden. Accordingly he struck out the clause and in doing so said to the Prince: "I count upon you, upon the King and upon the Swedish nation." The Letters Patent were accordingly completed containing a simple release of the Prince from his oath of allegiance, and the Prince is now in possession of them.'

Dr O'Meara, the author of *Napoleon in Exile*, stated that when talking about this affair of the Letters Patent while on the island of St Helena Napoleon said: 'I cannot say that he [Bernadotte] betrayed me. In a manner he became a Swede, and never promised that which he did not intend to perform. I can accuse him of ingratitude but not of treachery.'

Bernadotte spent about three weeks in Paris before he left for Sweden. He had not forgotten his famous friend Madame

Récamier whom, he realised, he would not see very often in the future. He wrote her a farewell letter:

> 'Madame—When leaving France forever, I deeply regret that your absence from Paris makes it impossible for me to take your commands and to bid you farewell. . . . Monsieur de Narbonne has been so kind as to undertake the duty of forwarding you my homage. We have often spoken of you, of your estimable qualities, and of the tender interest which you inspire in all persons who approach you. Farewell, Madame. Receive the assurance of the sentiments which I have consecrated to you and which neither time nor the icy North can ever extinguish.
>
> Charles Jean'

CHAPTER TWENTY-TWO

Crown Prince

On 30 September Bernadotte left Paris for Helsingborg where he received an enthusiastic reception on disembarking and made the following speech:

> 'Gentlemen, The Swedish King and nation have bestowed upon me a striking proof of their esteem and confidence. I have made every sacrifice in order to respond to it. I have left France which has always been the object of my existence until today. I have separated myself from the Emperor Napoleon, to whom a lively sense of gratitude and an infinity of other ties have attached me. It is not the hope of a crown that can compensate me for such substantial sacrifices. No, gentlemen: I shall find my true compensation in the happiness of my new country. I come among you, throwing everything aside, with an ardent desire to leave nothing undone that can contribute to your prosperity. I bring to the King, who is so deservedly beloved by you all, a boundless devotion. Let us unite, gentlemen, in the effort to fulfil his paternal wishes: and let us preserve unimpaired that national glory which you owe to the valour and the virtue of his ancestry.'

He was at once made Commander-in-Chief of all the Swedish armed forces and then left by road for the capital, a trip which took him nearly a month and during which he received a great welcome in all the towns and villages through which he passed. When he reached the Royal Palace in Drottingholm he had a most successful meeting with the king. His aide-de-camp Count Suremain said that His Majesty had told him that he had gambled heavily but really believed that he had won.

Having arrived in Stockholm on 2 November he was formally declared heir to the throne. In reply, he said:[1]

> 'Bred in camps, I bring you a frank and loyal heart, an absolute devotion to the King, my august father, and an ardent desire to do all in my power for my new country. ... I have seen war at close quarters and have seen its evils. Conquest cannot console a country for the shedding of her children's blood on foreign soils. I have seen the great Emperor of the French, crowned with so many victorious laurels, surrounded by his inviolable army, sighing for an olive branch of peace. Peace is the only glorious aim of a wise and enlightened government. It is not the extent of a State's Dominions which constitutes its powers and independence, but its laws, commerce, industries and national spirit. Sweden has sustained severe losses, but the honour of the Swedish name remains unspoiled.'

Bernadotte, who was in future to be known as Charles Jean, had said shortly after his arrival at Helsingborg that when he set foot on Swedish soil he had already become entirely Swedish. He soon became a popular figure and, according to a despatch sent by a British agent to H.M. Government, a powerful clique had approached him to displace Charles XIII by a coup d'état. Naturally he refused to have anything to do with it. He genuinely liked the king and queen and they liked him, because he could be attractive if he wanted; not only did they like him but so did the Queen Mother, who became very fond of him.

The Queen of Sweden made the following entry in her diary some two months after her adopted son's arrival.

> 'The King seeks every opportunity of showing his regard for the Crown Prince, and I begin myself to feel a high esteem for him. His manner and behaviour have gained my friendship, and the attitude which he has adopted towards the King cannot be sufficiently praised. A real son could not pay more attention and veneration than the Prince Royal does to the King. All his actions both to me and the King and to all his entourage are such as to win the affection of the people, and he is beginning to be generally beloved.'

Even the Queen Mother talked about 'Le Prince tout à fait aimable', and explained that when she said that Sweden had made a happy choice everyone should believe that she meant it since she was the mother of Gustavus IV.

In another despatch,[2] which was sent to the British Foreign Office, the writer stated that the prince behaved with rare circumspection and left nothing undone to captivate and please. 'The bigwigs', he wrote, 'do not know where they are with him because he says very little about affairs or about persons; and, as he knows nothing about the country, the reason of his reserve does him credit and tends to his advantage.'

Between October and December 1810 there were a number of differences between Bernadotte and his former Emperor, the most serious of which concerned Napoleon's Continental System, better known in England as the Continental Blockade, the object of which was to ban the import of all British and colonial goods to every country in Europe and to ensure a complete blockade of the British Isles. This obviously was most damaging to Sweden's commercial interests, for her trade with Great Britain was of great importance, and every effort was made to defeat the blockade. As a result of this, very soon after the Prince Royal's arrival in Sweden, an ultimatum was given to Sweden by Napoleon to the effect that if she did not declare war against Great Britain she would find herself at war with France. This was, of course, most embarrassing for Bernadotte but he was able to avoid having to take part in the decision whether or not to obey Napoleon's ultimatum.

Nevertheless, acting upon the advice of the Swedish Council of State, the King of Sweden declared war on Great Britain, but no one took it seriously. Immediately after the declaration of war Bernadotte wrote three letters to Napoleon, on 19 November and 9 and 19 December, protesting against the action which the Emperor had taken. In one of them he wrote 'When I decided to accept the succession to the throne of Sweden I hoped, Sire, that I should be able to reconcile the interests of the country which I had faithfully served and defended during thirty years with those of the country which had just adopted me. Scarcely had I arrived when I saw that hope destroyed.'

The blockade was, however, quite unsuccessful. The French ambassador at Stockholm was Baron Alquier who, very foolishly, on the instructions of Napoleon, wrote a letter to the Swedish Foreign Minister in which he accused the Swedish Government of 'treachery and falsehood'. The reply sent to Baron Alquier by the Swedish Foreign Minister was, in fact, dictated by the Crown Prince himself, and it left no stone unturned. The following is an extract: 'The climate of this country may doubtless disagree with you; and you may have formed a wish to seek another destination; but it was disloyal of you to provoke your removal by making assertions that are utterly groundless. . . . Those who are capable of the culpable design of provoking discord will always end by being unmasked.' This letter, followed by an audience which Alquier had with the Prince Royal, ended in the ambassador's dismissal.

The next question with which Bernadotte became involved was the relationship between Sweden and Russia. For some time there had been antagonism between the two countries about Finland which had belonged to Sweden until it was taken from her by Russia. It was hoped by a number of Swedes that when Bernadotte became Crown Prince he would help them to win it back. He had realised from the start that it would be a very foolish thing to do and he made it quite clear to those who were in favour of it that to undertake a war with that object in view 'would be a folly to which he would not lend a hand'.[3]

It was not long before the Czar of Russia, Alexander I, got to hear of this and he decided to use this opportunity to ensure that he would have friendly relations with the Crown Prince. Accordingly he wrote him a letter praising him for 'his talents, his character and his principles'. 'I desire not only your friendship,' he continued, 'but also your confidence. I wish for them because my esteem for you is of long standing and dates from the time when you were only a general. Brought up myself as a republican I have the happiness to value the man and not his titles. Do not allow yourself to be influenced by the fear of Russia with which people will try and impress you. The interest of Russia is bound up with the preservation of Sweden.'

Meanwhile trouble was brewing between the Czar and Napoleon and six months later the Emperor invaded Russia. The annexation of Norway was soon to become an important interest to the Prince Royal. This really began because his many supporters, who were disappointed in their hopes that he would win back Finland for them, expected him to create a united Scandinavia by acquiring Norway, which was then part of Denmark, and annexing her to Sweden.

Bernadotte also realised that he must try to persuade the Swedes that it was not worthwhile making Russia an irreconcilable enemy by trying to get back Finland, whereas the annexation of Norway was quite natural because it would join together the two countries which formed the peninsula of Scandinavia.

Bernadotte made an attempt to secure Napoleon's support but he was not successful, as will be seen from the instructions which the Emperor gave to his ambassador, in Stockholm, the Duke of Cadore.

> 'The project of acquiring Norway can be no more than a passing effervescence of the Prince Royal's imagination. He deceives himself if he supposes that Russia would consent to the transfer of that important province to her natural enemy. Besides, so long as Denmark is the ally of France, the Emperor will not be a party to any attack on her authority. No notice need be taken of these overtures. The Emperor is too strong to have any need of the concurrence of Sweden. You will say all this and you will take great care to preserve great dignity in your relations with the Prince. You will not speak to him about State affairs but you will address yourself upon those topics to the King or to the Cabinet.'

Napoleon, in doing this and in a number of other incidents which were not of themselves important, made Bernadotte's position in Sweden somewhat more difficult, which was precisely his reason. They removed or at least weakened certain links Bernadotte had with France which he had found it very useful to maintain. One of these links was his wife, Désirée who, while she was still in France, kept alive the friendly connection which he had with the rest of the Bonaparte family, most of whom liked him, in particular Lucien. Eventually there was really only one Frenchman in Sweden with whom Bernadotte was in close touch; his foster-brother Camps who was also a Palois, or native of Pau, and, like Bernadotte, a real Gascon.

Before long the situation was to become worse when in January 1811 Napoleon ordered Marshal Davout, who greatly disliked Bernadotte, to occupy Swedish Pomerania. The reason the Emperor did this was to set up a strong force to guard his left flank during the French invasion of Russia which was already planned to take place in June 1812. At the same time it did something to help the Continental Blockade which was not working satisfactorily; it ensured that no British ships could enter Pomeranian ports.

Bernadotte at once saw Napoleon's object in this move and he took immediate action. He sent a letter to the Czar pointing out why Napoleon had taken these steps, and urging him to take strong counter-measures. He ended his letter: 'In the midst of this universal despair, the eyes of men turn to Your Imperial Majesty with confidence and hope. Allow me to remind Your Majesty that there is nothing comparable to the magic of the first instant. So long as strength lasts success depends upon willingness to act. Those whose spirit is scared are incapable of reflection and yield to the force which terrifies or attracts them.'[4]

The Czar, in his reply, promised to send an envoy to Sweden and it was these negotiations which were soon to lead to the annexation of Norway. It took a long time for Napoleon to realise what a fatal mistake he had made when he invaded Swedish territory. He had imagined—as it turned out very foolishly—that the Swedes would have to depend on him and that he could get them to return to the fold whenever he decided to call them back.

Within six weeks of his invasion of Swedish territory Napoleon opened negotiations in Paris through the Swedish Consul-General, whose name was Signeul, with the Princess Royal of Sweden, i.e. Bernadotte's wife Désirée. The terms of the Emperor's approach were that Bernadotte should form an alliance with him against Russia which would necessitate the re-acquisition of Finland and the blocking of all trade routes with Great Britain. These terms were conveyed by Désirée to her husband. This led to nothing because all Bernadotte did in his reply was to offer his help in bringing about a state of peace between Russia and France. To try and make this suggestion a little more palatable he added the following extravaganza:

> 'Sire, one of the happiest moments I have ever experienced since I left France was when I was assured that Your Majesty had rightly judged my sentiments by recognising with what pain I contemplated the sad prospects of seeing the policy of Sweden on the eve of being separated from France, unless I am to sacrifice the interests of the country which has adopted me and has reposed in me an unlimited confidence. Although I am a Swede by the ties of honour, duty, and religion, my feelings still identify me with that beautiful France where I was born and which I have served faithfully since childhood. Every event of my life in this kingdom, and all the honours of which I am the recipient, remind me of that glory which was the principal cause of my elevation, and I do not disguise from myself the fact that Sweden in electing me wished to pay tribute of esteem to the French people.'

Sir Plunket Barton, *Bernadotte, Marshal and King*, states that this postscript was only written because Signeul, whose duty it was to take it to Paris, thought that the rest of the communication was 'too cold to move the Emperor'. Bernadotte who, while he was speaking to Signeul, was dressing in order to attend a meeting of the State Council, said, 'Very well, if you think it will help your mission, I will add a few lines. But let us make haste as I have to attend the Council.' Then 'while folding his tie', he dictated the passage quoted above.

Nothing of any importance happened as a result of the negotiations except that Napoleon is supposed to have said to a Russian emissary, who came to him from the Czar to talk about Sweden, 'As for the Swedes, it is their destiny to be governed by mad kings. Their King was mad. They changed him for another, Bernadotte, who promptly went mad, for none but a madman could, being a Swede, ally himself with Russia.'[5] On 23 June 1812 Napoleon invaded Russia. His invasion was, from the start, not very successful. The Russians carried out a planned retreat and never allowed themselves to be outflanked, whereas the flanks of the French Army were continually attacked by Cossacks.

Czar Alexander kept in touch with Bernadotte. Two letters written by him during the first six weeks of the campaign are of interest since they are evidence of the friendship which existed between them. 'I am playing the waiting game and am preparing to pursue a guerrilla warfare after the manner of the Spaniards in the Peninsular War and to defend the Riga in the spirit of Saragossa.' This letter was not dated. The second is dated 28 July. 'I beg Your Royal Highness to believe that I have often longed for your presence in the midst of my armies to guide the operations of this mighty struggle with your eminent talents and your great experience.... I expect to be in St Petersburg on the 20th where I hope to receive Your Royal Highness's reply, and I shall go to whatever place Your Royal Highness fixes as a rendezvous.'[6]

The meeting was eventually held at Abo which was at that time the capital of Finland. Alexander was very anxious that Bernadotte should take over command of the Russian armies but Bernadotte very sensibly thought that it would not be advisable for him to do so at this stage although he might do so in the future. The Czar wanted this not for any political reason but merely because, as he wrote in his letter, of the Crown Prince's 'eminent talents and great experience'.

Although at their meeting at Abo Bernadotte was still unwilling to take over command of the Russian armies, Alexander agreed to guarantee the annexation of Norway to Sweden; in order to help bring this about he undertook to land 35,000 men in Sweden between the following September and November to help in the conquest of Norway. Much more important than this undertaking, however, was the fact that the Czar and the Prince Royal got on very well together and as a result of this an alliance was formed between their two countries which was eventually to lead to the final defeat of Napoleon.

It may be wondered why Napoleon suggested that the negotiations in Paris regarding Finland should take place with the Princess Royal, since it would have been reasonable to suppose that by then she would be living in Sweden with her husband. She did, in fact, come to join him fairly soon after his arrival in Stockholm, but she very quickly found that life in the Swedish capital was very boring after her upbringing in Marseilles and life in Paris. Three months later she could stand it no longer and returned to France but left her son Oscar with his father. Her departure must have been rather embarrassing for Bernadotte as he was now heir to the Swedish throne and his princess would one day be queen.

It was not, however, merely embarrassing to Bernadotte, it was also very annoying to the Emperor who very much wanted someone to be with the Crown Prince. Who could be more suitable than his wife, for she was also the ex-fiancée of the Emperor and would ensure that the interests of the Bonaparte family were always kept well to the fore? So important was this that Napoleon did all he could to persuade her to return to Stockholm, but without any success.

While she was in Sweden in 1811 her health became affected by the very severe winter weather. This did give her some excuse to return to Paris which she liked so much and there she remained for the next twelve years until she returned on the occasion of her son Oscar's engagement to Princess Josephine of Leuchtenburg in 1823; she never again left her adopted country. While she was in Paris from 1811 to 1823 she bore, according to Sarah Lady Lyttleton, the courtesy title of the Princess of Gothland, had a town house in the rue d'Anjou and a country one at Auteuil. She kept in touch with Bernadotte and entertained all distinguished Swedish visitors to Paris.

But to return to the Russian campaign and the communications between the Czar and the Prince Royal. Bernadotte, in so far as all the available evidence shows, never had any doubts about the final result of the invasion of Russia whereas the Czar was very worried and greatly feared that St Petersburg would fall into the hands of Napoleon's armies. Bernadotte never even changed his mind when the news was received that Moscow had fallen, although the general opinion in Stockholm was that this made it certain that Russia would be conquered. There was so much misapprehension in Russia that Bernadotte wrote a letter to the Czar of which the following is a short extract:[7] 'Napoleon must be beaten in the end,' he wrote, 'because Your Majesty's armies can repair their losses and must always hold superiority in numbers, while his armies are at such a distance from their base that they cannot possibly count upon receiving reinforcements from Poland or from the interior of Germany.'

For a short time after the fall of Moscow there was a temporary cooling-off in the friendship between Alexander and Bernadotte, and at one time Bernadotte sent a message to the Russian Foreign Office saying that he had not thrown off the yoke of France for the purpose of submitting to the yoke of any power on earth. This was because the Czar had tried to withdraw his promise to send 35,000 Russian troops to Sweden to help Bernadotte to annexe Norway. At the end of December, however, when the retreat of the French army had become a rout, all was forgotten and from then onwards Bernadotte and Alexander remained on good terms.

Earlier in the year a very important conference had been held at Oslo which was attended by the Prince of Orange, three delegates from Russia, and four representatives of the British diplomatic service and the navy and army. Austria was also represented. One of the results of this meeting was a treaty between England and Sweden by which, inter alia, Swedish ports again became open to English trade.

When all this was going on something happened which, in the words of the French chargé d'affaires in Stockholm, 'produced the effect of a bombshell'. This was the arrival in the Swedish capital of Madame de Staël. Bernadotte was then able to renew his acquaintance with the 'mistress to an age'. When she arrived the Russian ambassador immediately called on her and offered to do everything he could to make her stay enjoyable. Her only reaction was to tell him that she was in need of no help as not only was she the wife of a Swedish baron but also a great friend of the Prince Royal.

She was an impossible woman, although she was very clever. She was said to be 'Swiss by origin, French by adoption, Swedish and Italian by her marriages, English in her political ideas and German in her literary tastes.'[8] A multi-racial woman if there ever was one.

She dedicated to Bernadotte her pamphlet on suicide, which was published about this time, in terms which were certainly fulsome and may or may not have been sincere.

> 'Until today I had dedicated my works to the memory of my father alone; I have applied to you, Monseigneur, to have the honour of doing homage to you, because your public life exhibits to all eyes those genuine virtues which alone deserve the admiration of reflecting minds. Among brave men you are specially distinguished for dauntless courage, but that courage is directed by a no less sublime benevolence. The blood of warriors, the tears of the poor, even the fears of the weak, are the objects of your humane providence, and the exalted rank in which you are placed will never be able to efface sympathy from your heart. A Frenchman used to say that you combined the chivalry of republicanism with the chivalry of royalty. Indeed, whenever generosity can operate it is ever in you an inborn quality.... Duties never seem to be a burden to you, but rather a staff; and it is for this reason that your habitual deference to the wisdom and experience of the King adds a further glory to the power with which he entrusts you. If you persevere, Monseigneur, in the career which offers you so splendid a future, you will demonstrate to the world something which it has not learned, namely, that those heroes are really noble who, far from looking down upon the rest of humanity, only think themselves superior when they can sacrifice themselves for others.'

The Prince Royal gave her a very warm welcome; she was naturally very grateful to him. During the whole of that winter she was one of the leaders of Stockholm society. She had an opportunity of meeting Sir Hudson Lowe who had come from England to make a report on the Swedish army. In his diary he described a meeting with Bernadotte at her house.

> 'We had the pleasure of dining with Madame de Staël yesterday. There, in a little theatre, Madame de Staël and her daughter went through some of the first scenes of Racine's *Iphigenia*. The Prince Royal entered soon, darting a glance at the company as he saw them collected in groups at small tables in the different rooms, and then glided away unperceived. I have never seen so remarkable a countenance as that of Bernadotte. An aquiline nose of most extraordinary dimensions, eyes full of fire, a penetrating look, with a complexion darker than that of a Spaniard, and hair so black that the portrait painters can find no tint dark enough to give it its rightful hue; it forms a dusky protuberance round his head, and he takes great pains, I understand, to have it arranged in proper form.'

In December 1812 the Czar and Bernadotte were both in agreement that steps should be taken to negotiate a tripartite alliance with England. The only difficulty was over the question of taking Norway from Denmark and annexing her to Sweden. For some time this proved insurmountable but Lord Castlereagh, who was at first against such an annexation, was eventually persuaded by Sir Edward Thornton, the British ambassador in Stockholm, that it was essential to the conclusion of an alliance with Sweden.

Early in March 1813 a treaty was signed between England and Sweden in the following terms:

1. Sweden undertook to provide 30,000 men as re-inforcement of an army which was about to open a campaign in northern Germany under command of the Crown Prince.

2. England agreed to the union of Norway and Sweden, and to pay in monthly instalments the sum of £100,000 to help towards the upkeep of such an army.

3. England agreed to give possession of the West Indian island of Guadeloupe to the royal Bernadotte dynasty.

Castlereagh wrote to Bernadotte immediately after the signing of the treaty. The last paragraph of this letter ran: 'Entreating Your Royal Highness to accept the tribute of my respectful good wishes for your personal glory and prosperity, in which I consider the best interest of the world to be at the present moment involved, I remain, with great deference and consideration, Your Royal Highness's most obedient and humble servant, Castlereagh.'[9]

Very shortly after the treaty was signed the French ambassador was asked to leave Stockholm and six weeks later France retaliated by getting rid of the Swedish ambassador in Paris. When the Swedish ambassador was told to return to Stockholm he was given a letter from Napoleon to the Swedish Foreign Secretary which tried to make trouble between the Crown Prince and the Swedish people and government by hinting that he was acting purely because of ambition and his hatred of Napoleon.

A reply was sent by Bernadotte which ended as follows:

'I was born in that fair France which you, Sire, govern. Its glory and its prosperity can never be indifferent to me. But though I shall never cease to desire the happiness of France I will defend with all my strength the rights of the people who have invited me to the succession of their throne, and the honour of the Sovereign who has deigned to call me his son. In state affairs, Sire, there is no room for personal hatred or affection, there are only duties towards the people whom Providence has called us to govern. Concerning my personal ambition, it is great, I confess. It is an ambition to serve the cause of humanity and to ensure the independence of the Scandinavian peninsula. To accomplish these ends I rely on the justice of the cause which the King has ordered me to defend, on the constancy of this nation, and on the loyalty of our allies. Whatever may be your determination, Sire, relative to peace or war, I shall none the less preserve towards Your Majesty the sentiments of an ancient brother in arms.'

Napoleon tried to pretend that he never received the letter but there is ample evidence that it was delivered to him. In any event the final rupture between France and Sweden was shortly to take place, presumably because Bernadotte had accepted the appointment of Commander-in-Chief of the army which was about to take part in a campaign against Napoleon.

CHAPTER TWENTY-THREE

The War of Liberation

The new campaign is generally known as the War of Liberation. It ended in October 1813 with the defeat of Napoleon at the battle of Leipsig and it had begun with Bernadotte embarking with his Swedish army at the port of Carlskrona.

It was most important that he should win this campaign, because if he did not the annexation of Norway could not be achieved. He must have had some doubts as to whether he would be successful, although he told the Russian ambassador in Stockholm that he had never been unlucky. The campaign was certainly a success in so far as Sweden was concerned, for it gave her a peace which has continued until this present day.

While Bernadotte was still waiting in the port of Carlskrona to equip his army before its embarkation, he was visited by two people who had been sent to persuade him to take certain action. The first of them was Colonel Pozzo di Borgo, a Corsican by birth who was supposed to have been a friend of Napoleon Bonaparte when he was quite a young boy. A real Corsican vendetta later grew up between them which according to local gossip had originated in their quarrelling over a bowl of soup. It is most unlikely that there is any truth in this story; the real cause of the enmity between the Bonapartes and the di Borgos was probably because in 1793 the Bonapartes joined the revolutionaries while the di Borgos were against the revolution and, with other Corsican opponents, managed to turn their island into a protectorate of Great Britain for two years.

After Corsica's reoccupation by the French, Pozzi di Borgo became a refugee in various countries, finally in Russia. He was apparently a remarkable man and Czar Alexander used him occasionally as what he called a 'roving diplomat'. The whole object of di Borgo's mission was to try to get Bernadotte to delay the attempt to annex Norway and concentrate on helping the Russians, with the assistance of Prussia, to drive Napoleon out of both countries. Di Borgo was unsuccessful. Bernadotte could not be persuaded to divert his forces.

On the very next day another envoy arrived. This time it was a Swedish officer named Colonel Peyron who brought a message for Bernadotte from Napoleon, and a letter from Désirée. The message from Napoleon was still another effort to dissuade Bernadotte from annexing Norway and do nothing more than occupy and defend Swedish Pomerania.

The letter from Désirée was to inform her husband of something of which he was already convinced—namely that the downfall of Napoleon was not far off, and to give him the following warning: 'If you declare yourself against the French you will lose the popularity which you enjoy among them. If Napoleon should fall you might play a great role in France and you might be the arbiter of a regency.'[1]

About this time rumours were spreading around Sweden that Bernadotte was in secret communication with Napoleon. These rumours were not, in fact, believed by any of those in authority, including the King of Sweden and the Czar, both of whom realised that the Crown Prince was by then entirely committed to his new country and that even had he wanted to betray Sweden—which in fact he did not—he could not have done so.

Bernadotte was, however, annoyed with both the Czar and the King of Prussia because neither of them had sent him the troops which they had promised him. The Czar only sent Bernadotte 4,000 cavalry when he had promised to let him have not less than 35,000. The King of Prussia did not send him any. In July 1813, just before Bernadotte left for Trachenburg to take part in the campaign which, it was hoped, would lead to the downfall of Napoleon, Sir Charles Stewart arrived at Swedish headquarters to which he had been appointed as Great Britain's representative in the War of Liberation. His brother Lord Castlereagh had already arrived at the Prussian Court as British ambassador.

Sir Charles Stewart dined with Bernadotte on the day of his arrival, and was not impressed with the Crown Prince at this first meeting, although he was later to change his views to some extent. On the morning after his arrival he wrote to his brother Lord Castlereagh, giving his very first impressions.

> 'The Prince Royal [he wrote] strikes me as being thoroughly French, cœur et l'âme. His engaging manners, his spirited conversation, his facility of expression and the talents which were perceptible even on a first interview, made no great impression on me, because I was prepared to meet all this. I rather regarded him as a highly finished actor; and I doubt whether he is, in the long run, a character either to admire or confide in. . . . The shifts and adroitness he can display, and possesses, would make me, even when sure of him, on the qui vive. I may judge him harshly but I never can look up to him nor shall I ever think him sterling till I see him spill Swedish in drawing French blood. . . . England will retain him as long as it is to their advantage to be retained, but there is no natural link between him and his allies. . .'[2]

It is quite evident, however, that although Bernadotte was French by birth he was even more anxious than any of his allies to bring about the final defeat of Napoleon, and it was essential for his future that he should succeed in doing this.

On 5 June an armistice had been signed at Plessnitz. The conference of the allies held at Trachenberg in Silesia at which, according to a report sent to the British Foreign Office by Lord Cathcart, 'the plan of campaign proposed by Bernadotte was agreed to'.

The plan, outlines of which were set out in Lord Cathcart's despatch, was as follows. Two armies were to be used, the Army of Bohemia and, operating in northern Germany, the Army of the North, consisting of 120,000 men commanded by the Crown Prince of Sweden. If either of these armies were attacked by the French the other was to advance on the attacking army from the rear. It was also arranged that the two armies should advance on Leipsig where it was intended the final battle should take place.

When the armistice ended on 10 August Berlin was attacked by a force of 70,000 men under the command of Marshal Oudinot. Napoleon's plan was for Oudinot to hold up the Crown Prince who was advancing towards Berlin while another French army under Marshal Davout, based on Hamburg, was to prevent his retreat to the sea and to Sweden.[3] By 12 August Bernadotte had reached Oranienburg, only about twenty miles south of Berlin, where he waited for Oudinot to attack him. The attack took place but it was a complete failure; Bernadotte, joined by the Prussian General von Bülow, defeated the French Army, inflicting about 20,000 casualties.

This was a great disaster for Napoleon and there was more trouble on the way. Within two months, on 19 October 1813 the Crown Prince entered Leipsig after a complete victory.

Before the successful battle of Leipsig, however, there had been some difficulties between Bernadotte and von Bülow who had wanted the Crown Prince to come up and guard his left flank. The other allied generals concerned appear to have supported the Prussian, including Sir Charles Stewart. There was a lot of argument before Stewart eventually won the day and persuaded Bernadotte to do what von Bülow had suggested.[4] A couple of years later, when Napoleon was on St Helena after being defeated at the Battle of Waterloo, he condemned his former Marshal for having given the allies the key to his policy and military tactics, and for thus having opened the way to France.[5]

CHAPTER TWENTY-FOUR

The Union of Norway and Sweden

The victory of Leipsig gave Bernadotte the opportunity to carry out the plan which he considered most important for his own country, namely to force Denmark to hand over Norway, which of course involved the invasion of Denmark by Swedish troops.

The following appeared in the *Quarterly Review* of January 1812: 'Each of the allies coveted a particular part of the spoil, and were willing to risk the fortunes of the whole alliance to secure it. Bernadotte wanted, in the first instance, Norway for his adopted country, and in the second, Napoleon's crown for himself. Alexander was resolved on seizing the whole of Poland . . . and, at the same time, securing for himself lasting influence at the Tuileries by selecting Bernadotte, instead of Louis XVIII, to replace Napoleon.'

Bernadotte lost no time in advancing towards the Danish frontier via Hanover, a city that was very glad to see him again as they had pleasant memories of his occupation of Hanoverian territory in 1805–6. Before actually invading Denmark, however, an Austrian diplomat was sent by Sweden and her allies to try to persuade the Danes to hand over to Sweden the Norwegian province of Trondhjem. If the Danes had agreed it would not have been necessary for Bernadotte to invade Denmark and he could then have joined his allies who wished to continue the battle against Napoleon, although he himself was in favour of a cessation of hostilities. However, the Danes refused and Bernadotte crossed their frontier; by January 1814, after he had taken Kiel and occupied Schleswig, the Danish government surrendered and the Treaty of Kiel was signed. Norway was ceded to the King of Sweden. In return Swedish Pomerania and the island of Rugen were handed over to the King of Denmark.

Bernadotte was most grateful to Czar Alexander for having finally agreed to his carrying on with the invasion of Denmark when the other allies had wanted him to join them in continuing the advance against the French armies. The Czar, in reply, tried to tempt Bernadotte to do this, now that the Treaty of Kiel had been signed, by suggesting that it might conceivably result in his finding himself on the throne of his native country. This suggestion was made in a letter which the Crown Prince received from the Czar. 'The decisive blows have been struck,' he wrote. 'France will soon have to fix her destinies. You will be the mediator between her and Europe and who knows where a happy star may lead you.'

What was Bernadotte's mental reaction to this suggestion? There is no doubt that to become the Emperor of France was always a dream, but it was really nothing more. One thing is certain—the dream never affected his plans, as he had maintained from the first moment when he arrived in Sweden in October 1810 that the duty which he owed to his newly acquired home would always come first and foremost. Nevertheless he did, before himself taking part in the invasion of France, try to persuade his allies not to do so because, as he told Sir Charles Stewart, he still desired peace with the French nation which he loved.

Three weeks later, however, having occupied Cologne

and then crossed the Rhine, he issued the following proclamation:

'Frenchmen, I took up arms by the order of my King to defend the rights of the Swedish people. Having avenged the affronts which they received, and having joined in the deliverance of Germany, I have crossed the Rhine. The vision of that river on the banks of which I have so often fought victoriously on your behalf, impels me to express to you my innermost thoughts. All enlightened men cherish the wish to see France preserved. Their only object is to prevent her from continuing to be the scourge of the world. The Sovereigns have not joined in a coalition in order to make war on any nation, but in order to force your government to recognise the independence of the states. These are their sentiments for the sincerity of which I am to you their surety. The adopted son of Charles XIII, placed by the choice of a free people on the steps of the throne of the great Gustavus, I can have in the future no ambition except to work for the prosperity of the Scandinavian Peninsula. Would that I might succeed, while discharging that sacred debt to my new country, in contributing at the same time to the happiness of my former compatriots.'

It was a most unfortunate proclamation to have made since not only was it of no help to him, in so far as the French were concerned, but it did not please his allies who certainly did not share his wish to see France preserved. The Czar and Lord Castlereagh, however, quite understood why Bernadotte would not take part in the invasion of France. As a compromise he remained at Liége for a month where he set up his headquarters while his Russian and Prussian troops continued to advance towards Paris.

It was while he was at Liége that a letter was brought to him from his brother-in-law Joseph Bonaparte stating that Napoleon wanted to know what Bernadotte was going to do. Bernadotte told the envoy who had brought the letter to give his brother-in-law the following reply:

> 'You can tell my brother-in-law that I know Napoleon too well not to see a trap in whatever comes from that quarter. I am sure that he either wishes to deceive me or that he deceives himself. My answer to his question as to what course I shall take is to advise him as to the part he should play—namely, to make peace as soon as possible. He can assure the Emperor that it is not to serve my personal interests that I give him this advice. It is on his account more than on mine that I advise him to make peace, although I know very well that I have always been the subject of his secret hate, because he has always misjudged me.'[1]

For some time Bernadotte had been in touch with several of the Bourbon princes, including the future Louis XVIII, who, when Bernadotte had gone to Sweden, thought that he might be helpful in bringing about the restoration of the Bourbon dynasty. After Napoleon's defeat at Leipsig these approaches were renewed by the Prince de Condé who offered to make Bernadotte generalissimo of the French armed forces if he succeeded in bringing the Bourbons back to the throne of France.

This was not enough to tempt Bernadotte, but there is little doubt that he was rather disappointed when he first heard the news that the allies had entered Paris. Nevertheless, he was not going to show his disappointment and wrote to the Prince expressing his delight at the probability of a Bourbon once again becoming King of France.

'My cousin, the Comte de Bouille, has handed me the letter which you have done me the honour of writing to me. I am infinitely sensible of all the agreeable things which it contains, and I beg Your Highness to accept my sincere thanks. Yes, it is glorious to contemplate the possibility of uniting in the cause of the happiness of our land of birth, and I abandon myself to the hope of seeing the successor of Henri IV re-established on the throne of France. There is also consolation in the prospect of seeing the end of the numberless calamities which for so many years have afflicted our ancient and unhappy country. I am not blind to the fact that, although the allies are already masters of the capital, there are still great difficulties to overcome before the goal is reached, because of the despair to which Bonaparte is reduced.'

This was written in 1814. Almost immediately afterwards Bernadotte had to return urgently to Sweden as certain difficulties had arisen regarding her position with Norway, but before he did so he went to Paris. Various suggestions have been made as to his reason for doing so but there seems to be no doubt that it had nothing to do with the possibility of his succeeding Napoleon. It appears that the main reason was to take the necessary steps to ensure that the terms of the Treaty of Kiel should be obeyed. He was only in Paris for a couple of weeks and he never visited the land of his birth again.

When he arrived in Stockholm early in June he received an enthusiastic welcome, which was described by the British ambassador. Bernadotte, according to his despatch, 'was received with every demonstration of joy, the feelings of the people towards him having been raised to the highest pitch of enthusiasm'. He found a difficult problem facing him which was of considerable urgency. Although under the Treaty of Kiel the Kingdom of Norway was ceded to Sweden, the Norwegians objected to annexation which they maintained could not be effected without the consent of the people. Prince Christian Frederick of Denmark was appointed Regent but his reign, if such it could be called, only lasted six months. He formed an army of some 50,000 to prevent the annexation. It thus became necessary for Swedish troops under the command of the Crown Prince to invade the country. There was no actual fighting and Prince Christian gave up his regency and returned to Denmark. The Norwegian parliament, known as the Storthing, then unanimously elected Charles XIII as King of Norway, and Bernadotte became its Crown Prince.

After this problem had been satisfactorily solved, Bernadotte, for almost the first time in his life, had an opportunity to relax. As one of his biographers has written 'his aspirations were satisfied and his ambitious nature was at rest'.[2] He had also completely won over his fellow countrymen. Bernard Sarrans wrote of him: 'The Swedes were grateful and appreciative when they saw this French warrior, this ex-general of the epoch of the Republic, this ex-marshal of the epoch of Napoleon, lavishing upon their aged and infirm king the most tender and delicate attentions, adapting all his habits to suit those of his adopted father, and winning the affection not only of both the Vasa Queens, but even of the Princess Sophie Albertine, great-aunt of Gustavus IV.'[3]

CHAPTER TWENTY-FIVE

The End of Napoleon

During the Congress of Vienna Bernadotte had been rather upset because all the representatives of the countries which were his allies did not more openly express their gratitude to him for all he had done for them in the past three years. England and Russia, however, stood by him, especially the Czar who stated emphatically that whatever anyone else might think about Bernadotte, he would always remember him with gratitude and respect. This pleased the Crown Prince very much and he wrote to express his thanks: 'Elected by the States-General of Sweden, and adopted by the King, I am fortunate in being able to add to my title-deeds Your Majesty's friendship and the honour of having retrieved the glory of Sweden.'

It was while the allied sovereigns and ministers were still assembled in Vienna for the Congress that it was learnt on 7 March 1815 that Napoleon had returned to France. When Bernadotte heard that the Emperor had landed in the Gulf of Juan he was by no means alone in thinking that there was not the slightest chance that he would ever reach Paris, but he did, and without even a shot being fired.

Everybody knows what happened after that. Napoleon decided to organise a campaign with Brussels as its objective because it was more likely than any other action to rally the support of France. The reason for this has never been described better than by the distinguished English historian, H. A. L. Fisher.

> 'For centuries, seeing that it brought with it the great estuary of the Rhine, Belgium had possessed a symbolic, almost mysterious value in the eyes of the French people. Over and over again the soil of this little country had been watered with French blood, nor had the ambition to acquire it ever failed to haunt the imagination of French statesmen. As the conquest of Belgium had been the first and principal glory of the young French Republic, and its loss the most damaging commentary on the Empire, so its recovery now would be a prize than which none could be more welcome to the heart of France. Napoleon, then, was right to strike for Brussels, and Wellington, taking station on the field of Waterloo, was right to deny the road.'[1]

Wellington called his army 'the worst-equipped army with the worst staff ever brought together', and it consisted of only 23,900 British, 17,000 Belgian and Dutch, 11,000 Hanoverian, 5,900 Brunswicker and 2,800 Nassauer troops. Powerfully reinforced towards the end of the day by the Prussian army under the command of Blücher, it completely defeated and routed the French, and the Hundred Days were over. The Corsican Ogre, as he had begun to be called, was exiled to St Helena and Louis XVIII restored to the throne of France.

Bernadotte did not really approve of the restoration of the Bourbons either before or after the Hundred Days, but he took care not to become involved in any of the plots to overthrow them. On the other hand, however, plots were made against him by the new French government, the intention of which was to get rid of 'the parvenu Prince' as they called him. Nothing came of them and as King Charles XIII approached the end of his reign the Crown Prince became all the more popular with his fellow subjects in both the Scandinavian kingdoms.

When his son Oscar reached the age of twenty-one he took his seat in the Council of State. He had learned his new language extremely well and was liked by everyone. At the ceremony in the Council of State, at which Oscar took the formal oath of allegiance, his father made a speech during which he addressed his son as follows:

> 'In preparing you for the rank to which you are called I have principally insisted on the study of history, which has made you familiar with the origin and source of princely titles, and the means by which they are maintained or destroyed. Your studies must have convinced you that it is the duty of a Prince to justify his rank by conspicuous virtues and superior qualities; that the admiration of his people is to be won by actions which are great, and their love by actions which are good.'

It must have been a great pleasure for the young man and his father to hear the speech which King Charles XIII made upon the same occasion.

> 'My age and infirmities [he said] disable me from giving adequate expression at this solemn moment to the thoughts which are prompted by my long experience of life and by my tender affection for you. I shall only remind you that one day you will rule over two free peoples. Prove to them by respecting their rights, the way in which you expect them to respect yours. Do not forget, dear grandchild, that I impose upon you today a sacred duty, namely, to repay, when I am gone, the debt which I owe your father for

the kind attentions and for the untiring tenderness which he has lavished on me from the day that he united his lot with that of this country. Always be to him what he has been to me. Be his support as he has been mine. Render to him all the care and all the consolation which he has given to my old age.'[2]

Oscar's mother was not present on this occasion. She was still living in Paris and did not come back to live in her husband's adopted country until Oscar's betrothal, five years after Bernadotte had succeeded to the throne.

CHAPTER TWENTY-SIX

Charles XIV of Sweden

On 1 February 1818 the condition of Charles XIII, who had been very weak for some time, became much worse and four days later he was dead. Bernadotte became King of Sweden and Norway and he was received enthusiastically. On 7 February the king's solemn affirmation was read out by the Grand Marshal at a ceremony attended by all the Officers of State, the judges and the chiefs of the army and navy. The new Crown Prince then took the oath of allegiance and a short reply was given by the new king to an address which had been presented to him by a deputation from the Swedish Diet.

'Separated as we are from the rest of Europe,' he said, 'our policy and our interests will always lead us to refrain from involving ourselves in any dispute which does not concern the two Scandinavian peoples. At the same time, in obedience to the dictates both of our national duty and of our national honour, we shall not permit any other power to interfere in our internal affairs.'

In Norway too there was enthusiasm on his accession to the throne although there was a demonstration by the peasants of Christiana who wanted to do away with the constitutional monarchy and have an absolute monarchy in its place. Bernadotte made it quite plain that he would countenance no such thing. In future he was to be King Charles Jean but members of the Parliament and all the Ministers of State and other officials when they took the oath swore to be faithful to 'their legitimate King, the high and mighty Prince and Lord, Charles XIV, Jean'.

In thirty-eight years Jean-Baptiste Bernadotte had risen from the ranks in the pre-revolutionary army of France to be one of the greatest of Napoleon's marshals, and finally a king and the founder of the Bernadotte dynasty which rules Sweden today. He still had to undergo two coronations and these took place at Stockholm and Trondheim on 11 May and 7 September respectively, both of them with all the usual pomp and circumstance. It is interesting, when considering the approval with which his accession to the throne was received in both countries, to remember the considerable impression he had made on several occasions previously when he was a French marshal. That he was such a success as King of Sweden is even more remarkable when it is realised that he never really learned to speak the Swedish language properly. Other countries, notably Great Britain and Russia, gave him welcome recognition. The Czar, in a letter of congratulation on Bernadotte's accession to the throne, paid him this compliment: 'The success with which Your Majesty has known how to maintain both your dignity and your glory under the most difficult circumstances is a sure warrant of the justice and wisdom which will mark the history of your reign.'

Louis XVIII's recognition of the new king, however, was only on the surface, it is possible that the Bourbon had some suspicion that Bernadotte was still in favour of a French republic, since there were rumours to this effect. It was, perhaps, for this reason that Bernadotte let it be known quite frequently that, in his opinion, for France to return to a republican government would be a great mistake and that the best thing for her, now that Napoleon had been got rid of, was a constitutional monarchy.

There was one thing, nevertheless, that Louis XVIII did for which Bernadotte was grateful. As has already been described, Désirée had been living in Paris ever since 1811 under her courtesy title of Princess of Gothland; in some quarters she had been suspected of being a secret agent for her husband. Louis however treated her with consideration and on several occasions gave her a private audience.

Now that Napoleon was in St Helena and had nothing better to do, he spent much of his time criticising his brother-in-law and former marshal. Although Bernadotte had made it quite clear to Napoleon that once he left France to go to Stockholm to become Crown Prince he would be loyal to his new country, Napoleon still reprimanded him for 'abandoning the Empire'. He also did his best to persuade Las Cases that the ex-marshal was not really pro-Swedish. 'If he had been a good Swede, as he pretended to be,' Napoleon said, 'he could have restored the lustre and power of his new country by seizing Finland and by descending on St Petersburg before I had reached Moscow.'[1] That was Napoleon's greatest complaint about Bernadotte, that he did not come to the Emperor's help during the Russian campaign. It should have been perfectly clear to Napoleon that as Crown Prince of Sweden he could not possibly desert his adopted country nor his allies.

The Marquis de Las Cases reported nearly everything which Napoleon had said about Bernadotte in the fourth volume of his book but it does not merit extended quotation because none of it approached the truth. Napoleon's views were a complete misrepresentation of what really happened. He said all these things because he knew perfectly well he would never leave St Helena alive; the bitterness which he quite naturally felt towards Bernadotte had cancered his mind.

When Napoleon died on 5 May 1821 Bernadotte said of him: 'He was the greatest captain that has appeared on the earth since Julius Caesar. If, like Henry IV, he had enjoyed the advantage of having a Sully[2] at his side, he might have regenerated Europe. If he was the greatest man of his age in his military conceptions, I surpassed him in method and calculation.' Bernadotte's final remark may, on the face of it, seem conceited, but it was not far from the truth.

From the commencement of his reign the new king's foreign policy was consistently built on the following principle: namely that he would not intervene in the affairs of any other nation unless, for some good reason, his own country could not help being involved. It was partly because of this that he gained and maintained the confidence and support of his subjects. During the first twelve years of his reign he did not have any great political problems. His place of residence was in Sweden and he only visited Norway when it was necessary for him to do so.

The Swedish constitution gave him a considerable amount of freedom. Although there was a small Cabinet which consisted of the Ministers of Justice and Foreign Affairs and four other Secretaries of State, he could, if he considered it necessary to do so, go against their advice. They were responsible to the Diet for the advice which they gave to the king, but he was not always obliged to take the advice so given, and the ultimate decision was in his hands. Whenever he decided to do this, however, he did not do it behind the Diet's back but would always call a special meeting to explain his reasons for making a decision which the Cabinet or the Diet had questioned. He would then do his best to get their agreement, but if he failed to obtain it he was quite prepared to proceed without it if he was convinced that it would be in the general interests of his subjects. Even later, when for the first time an opposition party was formed in the Diet, it gave him very little trouble until 1830 when a revolutionary cloud temporarily spread over Europe.

Norway, however, raised more problems for Bernadotte than did Sweden, for the constitution of Norway was somewhat different. The Storthing was more democratic and the only veto which the king had over it was a temporary one. He could suspend legislation being enacted by it but the suspension ceased to have any effect once the law had been passed by three successive sessions of the Parliament.

There were, nevertheless, other minor difficulties that arose although they would seem to be very petty. To give one example, the Norwegians wanted the late King Charles XIII and the new King Charles XIV to be known in Norway in future as Charles I and Charles II but outside Norway they would be called Kings of Norway and Sweden (as James I of England was also James VI of Scotland). Another matter on which there was a direct conflict between Charles XIV and the Storthing was when they passed a Bill for the abolition of the nobility. This they did twice and on each occasion the king refused to give his assent. In the end, however, he wisely gave way.[3]

One of the most drawn-out disagreements between the king and the Norwegian Parliament was on the somewhat sentimental but widely held opinion that Norway's National Independence Day should be held on 17 May instead of on 4 November. Bernadotte felt strongly that the proper date should be 4 November which was the day on which his predecessor had been proclaimed King of Norway. This argument went on until 1827 when it reached its climax and Bernadotte received a delegation from the Storthing to explain to them why he objected to 17 May. In a speech made to the Storthing on the subject he told them that in his long career there had been three incidents which had impressed him most painfully. 'The first,' he said, 'was when I was pressed to draw the sword against France, the country of my birth under whose banners I won the glory which was the principal motive of the Swedish people in choosing me for their throne. The second was when Norway, misunderstanding my benevolent intentions, forced me to invade her territory with an armed force. The third was in last year, when I learned that the Storthing had met to celebrate the 17th May.'[4] As a result of this speech the Parliament agreed that in future they would no longer celebrate 17 May. There was not complete agreement with this decision throughout the whole country and on the following 17 May there was a public demonstration by students in Christiana which was dispersed with no more than a few casualties. But this caused the Storthing to change their previous decision and 17 May was in future celebrated as the Day of Independence without any objection from the king.

Early in the 1830s Bernadotte began to have further difficulties with his Norwegian Parliament which, with a mixture of tact and firmness, he was eventually able to overcome. Simultaneously there was considerable opposition in Sweden in which the press played an important part. A new evening paper was started and the editor, named Hierta, was extremely revolutionary and made continual attacks on the king and in a most unpleasant way. Speaking to the Diet on the opening of Parliament Bernadotte had apparently told them that he considered himself 'the universal father of his people'. Hierta in an article pretended not to understand what the king meant and referred to 'the deep religious feeling which he had displayed by this touching reference to the Almighty'. It was, presumably, intended to be amusing but it could not have been more stupid as everybody else in

Sweden knew, as did Hierta himself, exactly what the king had meant, and that he had said it sincerely. The chief reason for the antagonism of the press to the royal family of Sweden, however, was the fact that some Swedish legislation gave the state certain powers over the press. They did not actually include censorship, but made it impossible for any newspaper to be published in Sweden without its proprietors first registering its title and obtaining official sanction from the government one month before first publication.[5]

The worst attack made upon the king, however, was by a Captain Lindeberg,[6] a journalist who had applied for a licence to open a theatre. The application had been turned down and Lindeberg then wrote a lampoon on Charles-Jean whom he called 'The King with the Long Nose', referring, of course, to the famous Béarnais nose which he shared with another famous Palois, Henry of Navarre, whose nickname was 'Nez Long'. For having written the lampoon Lindeberg was brought to trial on a charge of treason. He was convicted and sentenced to death.

Under Article 25 of the Swedish Constitution there was a most unusual provision that a person who received a royal reprieve could refuse it, and being quite convinced that the sentence of death would not be carried out in any event, Lindeberg refused to accept the reprieve and demanded that the sentence of death should be duly executed. No action to do this was taken and eventually on the twenty-fourth anniversary of his first landing at Helsingborg the king granted an amnesty to a number of condemned criminals who had been convicted of political offences or lése-majesté, including Lindeberg. He had no legal right to refuse this, and his sentence was then commuted to a period of detention for three years in a fortress.

During these early years of Bernadotte's reign, which were

by no means easy, his relations with England continued to be friendly, as he was determined they should be very shortly after he landed in Sweden to take up his position as Crown Prince and heir to the throne. According to a Foreign Office despatch 'he stated that his personal interest and feelings, as well as the commercial, geographical and political situation of Sweden, alike dictated a policy of cultivating the strictest alliance, friendship, and affection with England.'[7] The reason for this, he had once said, was because Sweden was the advanced post of England in the north of Europe, and without her all balance of power would be lost, which would mean the ruin of the secondary powers of Europe.

The revolutionary cloud which spread over Europe in 1830 was by this time in full swing. The restoration of the French monarchy had made little or no change in the condition of the French people. The old régime had disappeared forever and equality before the law, the liberty of the subject and the new judicial system which had been brought about by the Revolution of 1789 were not affected by the return of the Bourbons.

Decrees were enacted by Louis XVIII on 25 July 1830, limiting the freedom of the press, dissolving the Chambers of Parliament and altering the electoral system. This resulted in three days' fighting in Paris which ended the Bourbon dynasty. Louis XVIII was succeeded by what is generally described as the bourgeois monarchy of Louis Phillipe which lasted until February 1848 and was replaced by the Second Republic. In 1830 there was also a revolution in the Netherlands which brought about Belgian independence.

The Paris revolution of 1830, followed by the proclamation of Louis Phillipe as the new monarch, was an embarrassment to Bernadotte because it was not approved by the Czar although it was welcomed by England. Alexander intended to 'inflict condign punishment upon the insolvent democracy of France', and the only thing that prevented him from doing so was the outbreak of another insurrection in Poland.

Immediately after Louis Phillipe's election to the throne the son of Marshal Ney arrived in Stockholm with a letter for Bernadotte from the French king asking him to recognise Louis Philippe as the lawful King of France. Fortunately the Czar decided to recognise the new king which then enabled Bernadotte to do the same.

After this the relations between France and Sweden greatly improved and Bernadotte began a new friendship with Pau, the town of his birth, which Sweden has maintained to the present time. He kept in touch with it and the magistrates named one of their streets after him. This was a great change, for until then many people had regarded him as a traitor to his country since he left France to go to Sweden. This new mood spread from his native Béarn to Paris, where his name was inscribed on the Arc de Triomphe and a portrait of him was hung in the Galerie des Maréchales at Versailles. Finally, Thiers, who was the French President from 1871 to 1873, in a speech which he made in the Chamber of Deputies, excused him from any accusation of treachery by saying that 'when Bernadotte became Crown Prince of Sweden, he became a Swede unreservedly and must be judged from that standpoint.'[8]

There was one great difficulty which Bernadotte had in governing the country, namely the fact that he was not only unable to speak either Swedish or Norwegian properly but could not understand either language. At the opening of each session of Parliament he always had to make a speech which then had to be translated from the French in which he had written it. On one occasion he attempted to read the translation to the Diet but the result was so disappointing that he never did so again. It was amazing how he ever managed to carry on at all because government business had to be conducted with his ministers in French, the only language he could speak fluently. At the State opening of Parliament and on other important public occasions the interpreting was usually done by his son Oscar, who apparently did it so well that it is said to have made his father quite jealous.[9] It became necessary for all the members of the Diet to have a sound knowledge of French and there were one or two cases when a Councillor of State felt obliged to resign.

His memory, too, could be fallible. One occasion was most embarrassing when the king raised a matter before the Council of State to which he had already given his assent at a previous sitting of the House, although he had completely forgotten about it. Unfortunately for him it had been recorded in the minutes of the previous session and these were produced to support the Councillors' statement. The minutes had, of course, been signed by him.[10]

It is remarkable that despite all this his ministers admired him, had confidence in him and, what was more important, held him in great affection. He was moreover, a very hard worker and, like Winston Churchill, he did a great deal of his documentary work, reading reports and writing about them, during the early hours of the morning when he also frequently received his ministers. This habit, according to Christian Schèfer, is supposed to have originated in his days as a general in the French army when he frequently used to dictate orders to his staff officers while still sitting on his camp bed.

Perhaps his greatest virtue was his love of peace. Although he had been one of France's greatest generals it was truly said of him that he did not like war but knew how to make it.

In a Foreign Office document he was reported as saying that war had elevated him and that he had no fear of dangers, but that he felt it to be the greatest scourge that could be inflicted on any country, and that its brilliant successes could never be commensurate with the evils it entailed.

Just over four years before his death he was faced with a motion, moved in the Diet and supported by the coalition of the two opposition parties, calling upon the king to abdicate in favour of his son Prince Oscar. Bernadotte's reply to the motion was read to the members of the Diet by Oscar. In it he tried to remind them of the growth in prosperity which had come about since he first arrived in Sweden in 1810, about which an article had appeared in *The Times* on the very same day.

> 'The population of the Kingdom [it was stated in the article] was so much increased that the inhabitants of Sweden alone are now equal in number to those of Sweden and Finland before the latter province was torn from the former. The commerce and the manufactures of the country had been doubled, agriculture improved, instruction diffused, the finances raised from a state of great embarrassment to complete prosperity, the national debt almost paid off, a civil and penal code proposed for promulgation, the great canals which unite the ocean with the Baltic have been completed, and, lastly, the secular hostility of the Swedish and Norwegian nations has given way to mutual confidence, cemented by kindred institutions and the enlightened government of the same sceptre.'

The king's speech, while reminding the Diet that it would not be long before they got rid of him without his having to abdicate, concluded with the following appeal. 'Before descending into the tomb I appeal to you once more to understand your government.... When summoned, as I soon must be in the course of nature, to another life, I shall implore the benediction of the Creator for the two peoples who, when left to themselves, are adorned by so many virtues, and who have given me so many touching proofs of their affection and gratitude.' The opposition were unmoved by these words and after a bitter and most ungrateful debate a large number of members voted in favour of the motion.

Bernadotte was not going to be beaten, however, without fighting on, and during the next eighteen months during which the session still continued he eventually won the day, not however without some compromise. He had to agree that in future more real power would be given to the chiefs of the most important ministerial departments which would give them a greater influence in the Council of State.[11]

It had been a trying two years but when it was all over the king regained his former popularity. He became known all over Europe as the 'Grand Old Man' of Scandinavia, and in 1843, the twenty-fifth anniversary of his accession to the throne, there were general demonstrations in his favour in Stockholm and elsewhere throughout the kingdom.

The unpleasant and unnecessarily vindictive attack upon him during 1840 and 1841 had left its mark and from 1843 onwards he gradually weakened. In January 1844 he became seriously ill and died on 8 March, and was laid to rest alongside Gustavus Adolphus and his adoptive father Charles XIII who, ever since his adoption, had regarded Bernadotte as his own son.

Queen Desideria, as Désirée was entitled, not only survived him but also lived long enough to see her grandson on the throne, when he succeeded his father as Charles XV. She died in 1860, just fifty years after her husband had landed at Helsingborg before being elected Prince Royal.

References

PREFACE

1 André Maurois in his preface to a pamphlet published in 1966 by the Musée de Bernadotte in Paris and written by Gunner Lundberg, Cultural Attaché to the Swedish embassy in Paris.

1. BEFORE THE REVOLUTION, *pp. 1–6*

1 See the author's *Henry of Navarre*

2 Hochschild, *Désirée, Reine de Suede et Norvége*. Hochschild was Désirée's Chamberlain after she became the Queen of Sweden.

2. FROM NCO TO SUB-LIEUTENANT, *pp. 7–12*

1 Touchard-Lafosse, *Histoire de Charles XIV*

2 Wrangel, *Fran Jean Bernadotte's Ungdom*, Stockholm 1889

3. RAPID PROMOTION, *pp. 13–21*

1 *A History of Europe*, Arnold, 1936

2 *Memories*, Brussels 1848

4. THE SAMBRE ET MEUSE, *pp. 22–31*

1 Maurois, *A History of France*

2 Touchard-Lafosse

3 Sorel, *L'Europe et la Revolution Française*, IV

4 Touchard-Lafosse

5 Klöber, *Marschall Bernadotte, Kronprinz Von Schweden*

6 Sarrazin, *Biographical Sketch of Bernadotte*, 1812

References

5. A PERIOD OF DISCONTENT, *pp. 32–37*

1 Sarrazin
2 *Correspondence de Napoleon*, II, 1469, 1502

6. THE ARMY OF ITALY, *pp. 38–45*

1 Sir Dunbar Plunket-Barton, *Bernadotte*, 1914
2 Sorel

7. AMBASSADOR TO AUSTRIA, *pp. 46–52*

1 Masson, *Les Diplomates de La Revolution*, 1882
2 ibid.
3 ibid.
4 ibid. See also Dry, *Soldats Ambassadeurs sous le Directoire*
5 Masson
6 Dry

8. A MEMORY OF THE PAST, *pp. 53–55*

1 Barras, *Mémoires*, III

9. HIS MEETING WITH DÉSIRÉE CLARY, *pp. 56–58*

1 du Casse, *Roi Joseph*, 1855

10. MINISTER OF WAR, *pp. 59–70*

1 *History of France*
2 Touchard-Lafosse
3 *Le Moniteur*, 15 August and 4 September
4 Barras and Touchard-Lafosse

11. THE BRUMAIRE COUP D'ÉTAT, *pp. 71–78*

1 Touchard-Lafosse
2 Touchard-Lafosse, *Note Historique*, I

12. INTERLUDE IN PARIS, *pp. 79–91*

1 See Morrison, *Catalogue of Autograph Letters*

2 P.R.O.
3 Fisher
4 Herold, *Mistress to an Age*, 1959
5 *Souvenirs et Correspondence de Mme Récamier*
6 F.O., State Paper 26/62
7 Morrison

13. THE EMPIRE, *pp. 92–97*

1 Sieyès had voted for the execution of Louis XVI
2 *Lucien Bonaparte et ses Mémoires*, II

14. HANOVER, *pp. 98–100*

1 Pingaud, *Bernadotte, Napoléon et les Bourbons*
2 Klöber

15. THE GRAND ARMY, *pp. 101–102*

1 F.O., 64/68, Prussia
2 *Correspondence de Napoléon*, 9274

16. ANSPACH, JENA AND LÜBECK, *pp. 103–106*

1 *Correspondence de Napoléon*, 10318
2 A detailed description of the battle is given in Vol. 2 of Sir Dunbar Plunket-Barton's biography of Bernadotte
3 Houssaye, *La Campagne de Iéna*
4 Pingaud
5 *Correspondence de Napoléon*, 11250
6 Touchard-Lafosse

17. POLAND AND RUSSIA, *pp. 107–115*

1 For full details see Dumas, *Précis des Evènements*; Petre, *Napoleon's Campaign in Poland*; and the *Memoirs* of General Bennigsen.
2 *Correspondence de Napoléon*, 11737
3 Bennigsen, *Memoirs*, I
4 Zurlinden, *Napoléon et ses Maréchaux*

5 Bennigsen
6 *Correspondence de Napoléon*, 11855
7 Herriot, *Madame Récamier*
8 *A Selection of the Letters and Despatches of Napoleon*, 1884
9 See Plunket-Barton

18. THE HANSEATIC TOWNS, *pp. 116–121*

1 Plunket-Barton
2 Wrangel
3 Touchard-Lafosse; Pingaud
4 *Correspondence de Napoléon*, 14975
5 Dunn-Pattinson, *Napoleon's Marshals*

19. THE CAMPAIGN OF 1809, *pp. 122–126*

1 Pingaud
2 *Correspondence de Napoléon*, 15505
3 ibid., 15595
4 ibid., 15633, 15635, 15636, 15643, 15698
5 de Rocca, *Walcheren*

20. NAPOLEON VERSUS BERNADOTTE, *pp. 127–130*

1 Lecestre, *Lettres Inédites de Napoléon*, I
2 Touchard-Lafosse

21. THE THRONE OF SWEDEN, *pp. 131–142*

1 *Historiska Handelungen* (Swedish despatches)
2 ibid. Bernadotte later appointed the baron to be Viceroy of Norway
3 *Memoirs*, II
4 *Historiska Handelungen*, 263; despatch of Lagerbielke, 22 August 1810
5 Vassy, *Les Suédois depuis Charles XII jusqu'à Oscar I*
6 d'Ernouf, *Suremain*

7 *Historiska Handelungen*, 254, 255; despatch of d'Engenström, 21 August 1810
8 ibid. 265
9 *New Letters of Napoleon*. See also Lecestre
10 *Historiska Handlungen*, 303–4

22. CROWN PRINCE, *pp. 143–158*

1 Plunket-Barton
2 F.O., 73, 61–4
3 Plunket-Barton
4 *Correspondence Inédite d'Alexandre et Bernadotte*
5 Plunket-Barton
6 Both letters are taken from *Correspondence Inédite d'Alexandre et Bernadotte*
7 ibid.
8 Quoted, but with no source, by Plunket-Barton
9 *Lord Londonderry's Narrative*

23. THE WAR OF LIBERATION, *pp. 159–163*

1 Plunket-Barton
2 Alison, *Castlereagh and Stewart*, I; *Lord Londonderry's Narrative*
3 Holland Rose, *Napoleon*, II
4 *Lord Londonderry's Narrative*
5 O'Meara, *Napoleon on St Helena*

24. THE UNION OF NORWAY AND SWEDEN, *pp. 164–169*

1 Sarrans, *Histoire de Bernadotte*, II; Touchard-Lafosse
2 Plunket-Barton
3 Sarrans

25. THE END OF NAPOLEON, *pp. 170–173*

1 Fisher
2 Sarrans

26. CHARLES XIV OF SWEDEN, *pp. 174–185*

1 *Marquis de las Cases' Memoirs*, IV

2 See the author's *Henry of Navarre*. Maximilian Sully was Henri IV's right-hand man.

3 Schèfer, *Bernadotte Roi*

4 F.O., 73–132, 135

5 Plunket-Barton

6 Schèfer

7 F.O., 73–114

8 Pingaud

9 Plunket-Barton

10 Schèfer

11 F.O., 73–182, May 1840

Bibliography

BAIL, *Correspondence de Bernadotte avec Napoléon* (1810–14)
BARTON, Sir Dunbar Plunket, 3 vols. (1) *Bernadotte, the First Phase*; (2) *Bernadotte and Napoleon*; (3) *Bernadotte, Prince and King*
BENNIGSEN, General, *Mémoires*
BLOMBERG, Anton, *Le Maréchale Bernadotte*
BOURRIENNE, F. de, *Memoirs of Napoleon Bonaparte*
CAMBRIDGE MODERN HISTORY
COQUELLE, P., *Napoléon et la Suède*
CORRESPONDENCE DE NAPOLEON
DUVAL, J., *Napoléon,von Bülow et Bernadotte*
DUNN, Pattison, *Napoleon's Marshals*
DUMAS, General, *Précis des Evénements Militaires*
FISHER, H. A. L., *A History of Europe*
GIROD de L'AIN, Gabriel, *Bernadotte, Chef de Guerre et Chef d'Etat*
— *Désirée Clary*
HEROLD, Christopher, *Mistress to an Age*
HÖJER, Torvald, *Bernadotte*
HOSCHILD, Baron, *Désirée, Reine de Suède et Norvège*
KLÖBER, Hans, *Marschall Bernadotte, Kronprinz von Schweden*
LECESTRE, *Lettres inédites de Napoléon*
LONDONDERRY, Marquis of, *Narrative*
MARBOT, General de, *Mémoires*
MASSON, Frédéric, *Les Diplomates de la Revolution*
MAUROIS, André, *A History of France*
NABONNE, Bernard, *Bernadotte*
O'MEARA, Dr, *Napoleon in Exile*
PETRE, F. L., *Napoleon's Campaign in Poland*

Bibliography

PINGAUD, Leonce, *Bernadotte, Napoléon et les Bourbons*

RÉCAMIER, Juliette, *Souvenirs et Correspondence*

RICARD, General de, *Autours des Bonapartes*

ROCCA, de, *Walcheren*

SARRANS, Bernard, *Histoire de Bernadotte*

SARRAZIN, Général, *Le Philosophe ou des Notes Historiques et Critiques*

SCHÈFER, Christian, *Bernadotte Roi*

SOREL, Albert, *Europe et la Revolution française*

SUREMAIN, General de, *Mémoires*

TOUCHARD-LAFOSSE, *Histoire de Charles XIV*

WRANGEL, F. U., *Fran Jean Bernadotte's Ungdom*

ZURLINDEN, General, *Napoléon et ses Maréchaux*